HIDDEN GEMS OF THE REEF

HIDDEN GEMS OF THE REEF

Lesser-Known Species of Clownfish

ALINA HAZEL

Spectra Enterprise

CONTENTS

INDEX

INTRODUCTION

In the lively embroidery of coral reefs, where the kaleidoscope of marine life moves underneath the waves, the spotlight frequently falls on the alluring clownfish. These charming animals, deified by vivified movies and aquarium interest, are envoys of the sea as well as narrators of the unpredictable environments they occupy. While the famous picture of the clownfish frequently summons dreams of Nemo shooting among the limbs of anemones, there exists a domain of less popular species, the unlikely treasures of the reef, anticipating revelation and appreciation.

This excursion into the universe of less popular clownfish species is a journey of investigation, an odyssey that looks to disentangle the secrets, intricacies, and exceptional characteristics of these frequently disregarded marine diamonds. A long ways past the natural stories, these uncelebrated yet truly great individuals of the reef, with their particular ways of behaving, variations, and environmental jobs, add to the rich biodiversity and fragile equilibrium of coral biological systems.

As we set out on this campaign, we dig into the profundities of the sea to enlighten the unlikely treasures that embellish the reefs. From the logical complexities of scientific classification to the developmental stories that reverberation through time, from the unobtrusive subtleties of actual attributes to the perplexing trap of social ways of behaving, this investigation divulges the less popular types of clownfish in the entirety of their brilliance.

Scientific classification: Arranging the Uncelebrated Yet truly great individuals

Our process starts with the principal question of character, for inside the different domain of clownfish lies a large number of animal varieties ready to be ordered and perceived. Scientific classification, the study of naming and arranging life forms, fills in as the compass directing us through the maze of organic variety.

In the profundities of the coral reefs, where the light refracts into a heap of shades, the less popular types of clownfish anticipate ordered examination. Every species, with its novel morphology, hue, and biological specialty, frames a piece of the ordered riddle. From hereditary markers to morphological differentiations, the scientific categorization of these unlikely treasures unfurls, uncovering the complex connections that tight spot them to their marine domain.

Logical Order: Disentangling the Hereditary Woven artwork

Past the surface facade of varieties and examples, the logical order of clownfish includes a more profound investigation of their hereditary embroidery. The genome, a mind boggling code that holds the insider facts of developmental history, network, and variations, turns into a vital aspect for figuring out the unlikely treasures of the reef.

Logical grouping rises above the shallow and dives into the atomic complexities of qualities and hereditary connections. As we unravel the genomic code of these less popular species, a story unfurls — one that discusses normal heritage, difference, and the transformative strings that have woven these species into the unpredictable texture of the marine environment.

Transformative History: Stories from the Antiquated Reefs

The pages of the transformative history of clownfish resemble sections in an old adventure, where the heroes explore the always changing scenes of coral reefs. As we dig into the archives of time, we experience the less popular species as heroes in their own developmental stories.

The developmental stories of clownfish species, concealed in the fossilized leftovers of old reefs, uncover accounts of variation and endurance. From the shallow shores of ancient oceans to the many-sided labyrinths of contemporary coral developments, the transformative excursion of these unexpected, yet invaluable treasures reflects the powerful dance among life forms and their current circumstance.

Geographic Dissemination: Planning the Regions of the Inconspicuous

The immense spread of the sea disguises the geographic conveyance of the less popular clownfish species. Planning the domains they possess discloses a mosaic of submerged scenes, each with its exceptional arrangement of difficulties and open doors.

From the purplish blue waters of the Indo-Pacific to the isolated corners of coral-rich environments, these unlikely treasures cut out their domains. Understanding their geographic circulation becomes a cartographic undertaking as well as a window into the different living spaces and environments that characterize their reality.

Actual Attributes: Divulging Nature's Range

In the domain of clownfish, actual qualities are strokes on nature's material, each characterizing the one of a kind personality of an animal types. The less popular individuals from this family contribute their own tints and examples to the submerged show-stopper.

Unwinding the actual qualities of these unexpected, yet invaluable treasures uncovers the subtleties of their appearances as well as the useful transformations that empower them to explore the multifaceted designs of coral reefs. From blade morphology to tinge designs, every component addresses the developmental material whereupon these species have been painted.

Conduct Attributes: Exposing the Social Ensemble

Past the entrancing tones and shapes, the conduct characteristics of clownfish species make an ensemble out of friendly elements inside the coral reef environment. The less popular species, frequently ignored in this submerged ensemble, assume remarkable parts in the mind boggling dance of marine life.

Exposing the conduct attributes of these unexpected, yet invaluable treasures discloses the complexities of correspondence, settling ceremonies, and regional ways of behaving. From cooperative nurturing to perplexing romance moves, the conduct embroidery of less popular clownfish adds profundity to how we might interpret the social designs inside their networks.

Natural surroundings and Biology: Exploring the Submerged Mazes

The coral reef, a confounded universe of variety and interconnectedness, fills in as the living space and natural specialty for the less popular clownfish species. Exploring these submerged labyrinths, these unlikely treasures track down shelter, food, and a phase for the perplexing shows of life.

Investigating the environment and biology of these less popular species includes grasping their associations with coral arrangements, anemones, and individual reef occupants. From the formation of settling locales to searching methodologies, the unlikely treasures add to the biological equilibrium that supports the dynamic biodiversity of coral environments.

Protection Status and Dangers: Defending the Inconspicuous Fortunes

As mankind's effect reaches out underneath the waves, the protection status of less popular clownfish species turns into a basic concern. Evaluating their weakness and the dangers they face is fundamental for creating systems to defend these concealed fortunes.

From living space debasement to overfishing and the difficulties presented by environmental change, the less popular types of clownfish stand up to a horde of dangers. Understanding their preservation status gives the establishment to cooperative endeavors pointed toward protecting the fragile equilibrium of coral reef biological systems.

1. **Recap of Previous Chapters**

   As our investigation into the enthralling universe of less popular clownfish species unfurls, it is fundamental for stop and ponder the sections that have carried us nearer to the unlikely treasures dwelling in the profundities of coral reefs. Every section has been a disclosure, unwinding the many-sided strings that weave the story of these overlooked yet truly great individuals of the submerged domain.

   ### Scientific categorization: Unwinding the Personalities of Unexpected, yet invaluable treasures

   Our process started with the major investigation of scientific categorization — the study of order. In this section, we dove into the nuanced specialty of recognizing and classifying the less popular clownfish species. From the particular markings on their balances to the unobtrusive varieties in hue, scientific categorization filled in as our compass in exploring the different cluster of unlikely treasures that enhance the coral reefs.

Logical Grouping: Interpreting Hereditary Marks

Expanding upon the groundworks of scientific categorization, the section on logical characterization brought us into the domain of hereditary investigation. By translating the hereditary marks of these less popular species, we acquired experiences into their transformative connections and the complex embroidered artwork of their hereditary legacy. Logical arrangement turned into the way to opening the mysteries encoded in the qualities of these perplexing clownfish.

Developmental History: Reverberations from Antiquated Reefs

The pages of developmental history shipped us to the far off past, where the precursors of the unlikely treasures explored antiquated reefs. In this section, we followed the strides of these less popular species through ages and times, unwinding the stories of transformation, endurance, and the consistently changing scenes of coral biological systems. The developmental excursion of these clownfish turned into an immortal story scratched into the actual texture of marine history.

Geographic Circulation: Planning the Regions of the Inconspicuous

Geographic circulation arose as the map maker's material, showing the regions where the unlikely treasures have had a special interest. From the purplish blue spreads of the Indo-Pacific to the disconnected corners of coral-rich environments, we planned the differed scenes that act as the background to the existences of these less popular species. This section divulged the geological broadness of their living spaces as well as the interconnectedness that characterizes their appropriation designs.

Actual Qualities: Nature's Range Revealed

Plunging further into the visual orchestra of nature, the part on actual attributes uncovered the unpredictable subtleties that paint the unlikely treasures with nature's range. From the fragile examples on their bodies to the practical transformations that help their endurance, we wondered about the variety that exists underneath the surface. Each actual trademark turned into a stroke on nature's material, adding to the colorful excellence of these less popular clownfish.

Conduct Characteristics: Exposing the Social Ensemble

Underneath the waves, a social ensemble unfurled as we investigated the conduct characteristics of the unexpected, yet invaluable treasures. From the cooperative nurturing endeavors to the mind boggling romance moves, this part exposed the complex social elements that characterize the existences of these less popular clownfish. The submerged world, buzzing with correspondence, settling customs, and regional ways of behaving, turned into a phase for the unlikely treasures to assume out their extraordinary parts in the marine theater.

Environment and Nature: Exploring the Submerged Mazes

Exploring through the submerged mazes of coral reefs, we set out on an excursion into the living spaces and biology that support the unlikely treasures. From the making of settling destinations to rummaging procedures, we found the mind boggling dance between these less popular clownfish and their encompassing environments. This part given experiences into their biological jobs as well as highlighted the delicate equilibrium that upholds the lively biodiversity of coral reefs.

Protection Status and Dangers: Shielding the Inconspicuous Fortunes

As stewards of the submerged world, our process took an impactful turn towards preservation concerns. Evaluating the protection status and recognizing the dangers looked by the unexpected, yet invaluable treasures became foremost. From environment corruption to overfishing and the effects of environmental change, we defied the difficulties that risk the prosperity of these less popular clownfish. This part made way for cooperative endeavors pointed toward shielding the inconspicuous fortunes underneath the waves.

Recap: Disclosing the Charm of Unlikely treasures

With every part, the embroidery of unlikely treasures in the reef unfurled, uncovering a universe of charm, variety, and interconnectedness. The scientific classification and logical arrangement parts furnished us with the focal points to observe the personalities and hereditary accounts of these less popular species. In the passageways of transformative history, we heard reverberations from antiquated reefs, following the developmental excursions that have formed the unlikely treasures we experience today.

Geographic dispersion and actual qualities directed us through the changed scenes and visual exhibitions that characterize the living spaces of these clownfish. We then dove into the conduct orchestra, exposing the social elements that work out in the coral reefs — the perplexing moves, the correspondence modalities, and the helpful endeavors that characterize the existences of the unlikely treasures.

Exploring the submerged mazes of environment and nature, we found the imperative jobs these less popular clownfish play in supporting the fragile equilibrium of coral biological systems. The investigation of their preservation status and the dangers they face carried us up close and personal with the squeezing need for aggregate activity to safeguard these inconspicuous fortunes.

In this recap, we stand at the junction of revelation, furnished with information and a profound appreciation for the unlikely treasures that occupy the coral reefs. The excursion is not even close to finished, and the parts yet to unfurl vow to extend our figuring out, flash interest, and rouse a common obligation to the preservation of these less popular clownfish species. As we turn the page to the following part, we convey with us the charm of the unlikely treasures and a feeling of obligation to guarantee their accounts keep on resounding in the huge field of the sea's hug.

2. Importance of Ole in the Clownfish Family

Inside the tremendous and perplexing embroidery of the coral reefs, the clownfish family stands apart as a spellbinding and fundamental gathering. In the midst of this brilliant group, the less popular species, Ole (Amphiprion oleanus), arises as an unmistakable jewel, holding a one of a kind significance that adds to the general flexibility and congruity of the clownfish family. As we dive into the profundities of Ole's job inside this family, we find the complexities that make it a part as well as a cornerstone, forming the elements and biological equilibrium of the submerged world.

1. **Biological Agreement: Ole as a Messenger of Equilibrium**
   Ole, as other clownfish species, assumes a vital part in keeping up with the natural concordance of coral reefs. These dynamic submerged environments are sensitive and interconnected, depending on a fragile equilibrium to flourish. Ole, with its particular ways of behaving, scrounging examples, and cooperations with other reef occupants, turns into a messenger of equilibrium inside this complex snare of life.
   By adding to the guideline of prey populaces and taking part in mutualistic associations with anemones, Ole keeps up with the balance of the reef biological system. Its presence, ways of behaving, and collaborations structure vital parts of the environmental riddle, guaranteeing that the clownfish family, including Ole, fills in as a balancing out force inside the coral reef local area.

2. **Biodiversity Backing: Ole's Specialty in the Clownfish Range**
   The clownfish family contains a different cluster of animal varieties, each adjusted to its extraordinary specialty inside the coral reef climate. Ole, as a less popular animal types, possesses a particular natural specialty, adding to the general biodiversity of clownfish in these dynamic marine biological systems.
   Biodiversity is a foundation of environment versatility, and Ole, with its particular arrangement of ways of behaving, conceptive systems, and living space inclinations, adds a layer of intricacy to the embroidery of clownfish biodiversity. This variety isn't just a scene for submerged fans yet an imperative part that improves the versatility of the clownfish family even with natural difficulties.

3. **Regenerative Systems: Ole's Commitment to Hereditary Variety**
   The regenerative systems of Ole further stress its significance inside the clownfish family. As a monogamous animal categories that structures long haul pair bonds, Ole participates in ways of behaving, for example, home structure and parental consideration, adding to the propagation of its hereditary genealogy. This part of Ole's science isn't just captivating yet holds significant ramifications for the hereditary variety of the whole clownfish family.
   Hereditary variety is a foundation of transformative strength. By participating in monogamous organizations and showing parental consideration, Ole guarantees

the endurance and variety of its posterity. This hereditary variety, thus, adds to the flexibility and heartiness of the whole clownfish family, empowering them to confront ecological changes and difficulties over the long run.

4. **Social Elements: Ole's Job in the Clownfish People group**

   Inside the social embroidery of the clownfish local area, Ole plays a nuanced job that goes past individual endurance. The social elements among clownfish species include multifaceted orders, correspondence procedures, and cooperative ways of behaving. Ole, as an individual from this local area, adds to the social lucidness and useful elements that characterize the clownfish family.

   Through correspondence signals, regional ways of behaving, and helpful exercises, Ole fortifies the securities inside the clownfish local area. These social communications are interesting to see as well as serve imperative capabilities, like guard against hunters, agreeable searching, and shared insurance inside the coral reef territory.

5. **Mutualistic Connections: Ole and Anemones as Accomplices in Endurance**

   One of the trademark elements of clownfish, including Ole, is their mutualistic relationship with ocean anemones. This harmonious organization is a demonstration of the significance of Ole inside the clownfish family and the more extensive coral reef environment.

   Ole, similar to its clownfish partners, looks for shelter inside the stinging limbs of anemones, acquiring assurance from hunters. Consequently, clownfish give significant supplements to the anemones through their waste and safeguard them from expected dangers.

   This mutualistic relationship isn't just a striking illustration of coevolution yet in addition highlights Ole's importance as a facilitator of cooperative equilibrium inside the complex coral reef territories.

6. **Preservation Importance: Ole as a Flagbearer for Unexpected, yet invaluable treasures**

Past its natural jobs, Ole holds importance in the more extensive setting of marine protection. As a less popular animal categories, Ole turns into a flagbearer for the protection of unexpected, yet invaluable treasures inside the clownfish family. The consideration attracted to Ole's exceptional characteristics and the significance it holds inside the coral reef biological system fills in as an indication of the more extensive need to safeguard and protect less popular species that might be ignored in preservation endeavors.

Protection endeavors zeroed in on Ole stretch out past defending a solitary animal types; they add to the safeguarding of biodiversity, biological system flexibility, and the multifaceted connections that characterize the clownfish family. Ole's protection importance lies in its natural worth as well as in portrayal of the secret marvels add to the general wellbeing and imperativeness of coral reef environments.

C. Overview of Ole's Unique Characteristics

In the immense and various domain of clownfish species, Ole (Amphiprion oleanus) remains as an unlikely treasure — an animal groups with one of a kind qualities that recognize it inside the many-sided embroidery of coral reefs. As we set out on a top to bottom investigation of Ole's credits, we disclose a dazzling outline of its physical, conduct, and biological highlights that add to its cryptic appeal. From unmistakable hue and harmonious organizations to complicated social ways of behaving, Ole's novel qualities paint a representation of an animal groups that assumes an essential part in the submerged environments it calls home.

1. **Actual Attributes: Nature's Range Encapsulated**

    At the core of Ole's charm lies its actual qualities, a material whereupon nature has painted a hypnotizing range of varieties and examples. Not at all like its more prestigious partners, Ole brags a remarkable blend shades and markings that put it aside inside the clownfish family.

    1.1 Hue: An Ensemble of Tones

    Ole's hue is an ensemble of shades that reaches from lively oranges and reds to unpretentious slopes that dance along its body. Dissimilar to the notorious examples of some other clownfish species, Ole features a more quelled tastefulness, permitting it to flawlessly mix into the complicated coral conditions it possesses. This repressed shading fills a tasteful need as well as helps in cover, offering Ole a degree of security against likely hunters.

    1.2 Size and Morphology: Reduced and Deft

    As far as size, Ole falls inside the range commonplace for clownfish species. Its conservative body and smoothed out morphology add to its deftness, permitting it to explore through the complex designs of coral reefs easily. The smoothed out shape isn't simply a result of development; it is a demonstration of Ole's transformation to the complex territories it calls home.

    1.3 Blade Morphology: Exploring Submerged Labyrinths

    Ole's balance morphology is finely tuned for exploring the submerged labyrinths of coral reefs. The pectoral balances, specifically, are a key component, giving both dependability and accuracy in development. These balances fill double needs, empowering Ole to skim through the water with elegance while additionally supporting the perplexing moves expected for exploring the intricate geology of coral arrangements.

2. **Conduct Qualities: Social Elements and Correspondence**

    Past its visual allure, Ole's conduct characteristics add layers of intricacy to its personality inside the clownfish family. These ways of behaving envelop social elements, correspondence systems, and helpful communications that add to the species' endurance and outcome in its environment.

    2.1 Social Construction: Agreeable People group

    Ole, in the same way as other clownfish species, shows a social construction portrayed by helpful networks. Inside these networks, people structure various leveled connections that are essential for bunch union and endurance. Ole's job inside the social design includes cooperative endeavors in exercises like searching, an area safeguard, and security of the home.

2.2 Correspondence Systems: Visual and Substance Signs

Correspondence is a foundation of Ole's social elements, with people utilizing visual and compound signs to pass on data. Visual signs, including balance shows and body stances, assume a part in laying out strength, starting romance, and keeping social control inside the gathering. Moreover, synthetic prompts add to an area acknowledgment and mate determination, improving the mind boggling correspondence network that characterizes Ole's social cooperations.

2.3 Settling and Parental Consideration: Gatekeepers of People in the future

Ole's regenerative ways of behaving include many-sided settling ceremonies and parental consideration, adding profundity to its job inside the clownfish family. As a monogamous animal varieties, Ole frames long haul pair bonds, taking part in exercises, for example, home structure and protection. The cooperative endeavors of the male and female in monitoring and really focusing on the eggs feature the helpful idea of Ole's conceptive techniques.

3. **Environment and Nature: Exploring Coral Mazes**

Ole's environment and natural inclinations are basic parts of its remarkable attributes. As an inhabitant of coral reefs, Ole explores the mind boggling mazes of coral developments, adding to the elements of its biological specialty.

3.1 Anemone Connections: Harmonious Concordance

Like other clownfish species, Ole participates in cooperative associations with ocean anemones. The association among Ole and anemones includes common advantages — security for the clownfish inside the anemone's appendages and supplements gave to the anemone through the clownfish's exercises. Ole's choice of explicit anemone species mirrors its transformation to these advantageous organizations, which act as key parts of its biological job.

3.2 Scrounging Systems: Agreeable Hunting

Ole's scrounging systems underscore agreeable hunting inside the coral reef climate. As a feature of a local area, Ole partakes in facilitated searching exercises, boosting the effectiveness of finding and catching prey. The capacity to team up in rummaging tries adds to the general progress of the clownfish local area and highlights Ole's importance in keeping up with the environmental equilibrium of its living space.

4. **Preservation Status: Saving a Secret Fortune**

Understanding Ole's interesting qualities isn't just an issue of logical request yet additionally holds suggestions for its preservation. As a less popular animal varieties,

Ole faces preservation challenges that come from living space corruption, environmental change, and potential dangers related with human exercises.

4.1 Protection Concerns: Tending to Dangers

Ole's protection status is complicatedly connected to the prosperity of coral reefs, making it defenseless to the more extensive dangers confronting these biological systems. Territory corruption, coral dying, and disturbances in the perplexing equilibrium of the reef climate present difficulties to Ole's endurance.

Tending to these dangers requires comprehensive preservation methodologies that include both natural surroundings security and worldwide endeavors to moderate environmental change influences.

4.2 Protection Endeavors: Cooperation for Safeguarding

Endeavors pointed toward saving Ole and its living space require coordinated effort on numerous fronts. Preservation drives might incorporate the foundation of marine safeguarded regions, economical fishing practices, and local area commitment programs that bring issues to light about the significance of clownfish species, especially the less popular pearls like Ole. By cultivating a feeling of stewardship and shared liability, these endeavors add to the safeguarding of Ole as a secret fortune inside the marine world.

Chapter 1

Taxonomy And Classification

The world underneath the sea's surface is a mind boggling embroidery of life, a many-sided snare of species interconnected in manners that frequently evade the relaxed eyewitness. At the core of understanding this biodiversity lies the study of scientific categorization and order, a discipline that looks to sort out and classify the bunch types of life that occupy the watery profundities. In this investigation, we dive into the profundities of scientific categorization and grouping, disentangling the strings that tight spot the less popular types of clownfish, with a specific spotlight on the baffling Ole.

Scientific classification: A Plan of Variety

Scientific classification, frequently viewed as the plan of natural variety, is the study of naming, characterizing, and ordering life forms in light of shared qualities. An efficient methodology endeavors to carry request to the huge swath of living things, doling out them into various leveled classes that mirror their transformative connections. At the broadest level, scientific categorization coordinates living creatures into spaces, realms, and phyla, making a platform whereupon the better subtleties of order can be constructed.

The Developmental Odyssey of Ole

Inside the domain of clownfish, Ole sets out on a transformative odyssey that entwines with the more extensive woven artwork of marine life. Ole, deductively grouped inside the family Pomacentridae, class Amphiprion, possesses a one of a kind specialty in the developmental course of events. Its process can be followed through the chronicles of time, featuring the mind boggling associations with other clownfish species and revealing insight into the common family line that joins them.

Hereditary Signs: Opening the Mysteries of Relatedness

Progressions in sub-atomic science have become strong partners in the taxonomist's arms stockpile, offering hereditary signs that enlighten the multifaceted ways of transformative relatedness. On account of Ole, hereditary markers furnish bits of knowledge into its associations with other clownfish species and uncover the secret strings that tight spot them. By contrasting DNA successions, researchers disentangle the hereditary embroidered artwork that highlights the family ties inside the different universe of clownfish.

Geographic Dispersion: Planning the Clownfish Realm

Scientific categorization reaches out past the lab into the huge field of the seas, where geographic dispersion turns into a critical calculate order. Ole's presence isn't uniform across the world's reefs, and understanding its conveyance designs adds to a nuanced order. From the coral reefs of the Indo-Pacific to the little hiding spots of the Incomparable Hindrance Reef, Ole's geographic impression portrays its biological inclinations and transformations.

Actual Qualities: An Ordered Embroidery

One of the characterizing parts of scientific categorization is the grouping in light of morphological elements. Ole, as other clownfish, shows a dazzling exhibit of actual qualities that act as key markers for characterization. Its unmistakable tinge, size, and morphological subtleties make an ordered embroidery that separates it from its clownfish partners. The complicated subtleties of Ole's actual structure become the brushstrokes in the representation of its ordered character.

Pecking order of Grouping: Ole's Position in the Ordered Pyramid

Inside the various leveled system of scientific categorization, Ole has its spot as an animal categories, an individual from the more extensive class Amphiprion, and a delegate of the family Pomacentridae. Understanding this order gives a guide to Ole's ordered importance. Each degree of grouping implies a more profound layer of shared qualities and developmental history, coming full circle in the novel character of Ole inside the immense realm of clownfish.

Transformative History: Following Ole's Genealogical Roots

To genuinely see the value in Ole's position in the ordered scene, we should set out on an excursion through its transformative history. This story unfurls like a charming story, with Ole's progenitors exploring the old oceans, adjusting to evolving conditions, and cutting out their specialty in the unpredictable dance of hunter and prey. The exciting bends in the road of Ole's transformative excursion are carved in its hereditary code, a demonstration of the versatility and flexibility of the clownfish genealogy.

Communication with Other Clownfish: The Social Texture of Scientific categorization

In the domain of scientific categorization, the connections between life forms stretch out past simple arrangement; they become strings in the social texture of environmental networks. Ole's connection with other clownfish species adds profundity to its ordered story. Whether taking part in cooperative associations with anemones or exploring the sensitive dance of territoriality, Ole's social elements weave a story that rises above the bounds of grouping.

Scientific categorization in real life: Hands on work and Disclosure

The order of Ole isn't bound to research facilities and hereditary examinations alone; it stretches out into the field, where taxonomists leave on campaigns to notice these animals right at home. Hands on work turns into a residing research center, where the subtleties of conduct, nature, and ecological collaborations give extra layers to Ole's ordered profile. The powerful idea of scientific categorization is uncovered as researchers make new revelations and refine existing groupings in light of genuine perceptions.

Scientific classification and Preservation: A Call to Safeguard Biodiversity

Understanding the scientific classification of species like Ole isn't only a scholastic pursuit; it conveys significant ramifications for protection. As human exercises progressively influence marine environments, a careful comprehension of the scientific categorization and order of clownfish turns into a pivotal device for viable preservation methodologies. By distinguishing and safeguarding the novel specialties involved by Ole, we add to the conservation of biodiversity and the sensitive equilibrium of the submerged world.

Future Wildernesses: Unwinding Ordered Secrets

The excursion through scientific categorization and characterization is a continuous investigation, with numerous boondocks yet to be outlined. The arrangement of Ole, while revealing insight into its at various times, likewise suggests conversation starters for what's to come. What new species and connections anticipate revelation in the neglected profundities? How might propels in innovation and strategy refine how we might interpret the ordered scene? The unfurling sections of scientific classification guarantee an embroidery of revelation, with Ole as one of its unexpected, yet invaluable treasures.

1.1 Scientific Classification of Ole

The logical characterization of Ole, a less popular types of clownfish, uncovers a captivating story of developmental heredity, hereditary complexities, and natural transformations. As we analyze the ordered riddle encompassing Ole, we set out on an excursion through the progressive structure of characterization, investigating its position in the excellent embroidery of life.

Area: Eukarya - The Domain of Intricate Cells

At the most elevated level of logical order, Ole, similar to every living organic entity, has a place with the space Eukarya. This area envelops organic entities with complex cells, recognizing them from the prokaryotic cells tracked down in microbes and archaea. Ole's eukaryotic nature denotes the start of its ordered excursion inside the more extensive setting of cell intricacy.

Realm: Animalia - Embracing Multicellular Heterotrophs

As an individual from the animals of the world collectively, Ole is portrayed by multicellular association and heterotrophic nourishment. This realm includes a huge swath of living beings, going from minuscule spineless creatures to lofty vertebrates. Ole's place inside Animalia makes way for a more point by point investigation of its ordered character.

Phylum: Chordata - A Melody of Vertebrates

Inside the animals of the world collectively, Ole finds its spot in the phylum Chordata, a different gathering that incorporates vertebrates and a few firmly related spineless creatures. The characterizing element of chordates is the presence of a notochord, an adaptable pole that offers help during early stage improvement. Ole, being a vertebrate, shares this trademark with its fish family members.

Subphylum: Vertebrata - Spine of Ordered Character

The subphylum Vertebrata limits the concentration to creatures with an advanced vertebral segment or spine. Ole's consideration in this subphylum features its common family line with different vertebrates, stressing the primary significance of the spine in its ordered personality.

Class: Actinopterygii - The Beam Finned Fish

Ole, similar to all clownfish, has a place with the class Actinopterygii, which contains beam finned fish. Most of fish species fall into this class, described by balances upheld by hard beams. Ole's blades, embellished with lively varieties and perplexing examples, are meaningful of the actinopterygian genealogy to which it has a place.

Request: Perciformes - A Different Exhibit of Roost Like Fish

Inside the class Actinopterygii, Ole finds its spot in the request Perciformes, a different and broad gathering that incorporates a wide exhibit of roost like fish. Perciformes is one of the biggest orders of vertebrates, exhibiting the flexibility and developmental outcome of its individuals, including Ole.

Family: Pomacentridae - Embracing the Clownfish Family

As we tight our concentrate further, Ole has its spot inside the family Pomacentridae. This family is known for its stunning cluster of damselfishes and clownfishes, with Ole finding its specialty close by its more popular family members like Amphiprion ocellaris and Amphiprion percula.

The Pomacentridae family is portrayed by little size, lively hue, and the unmistakable way of behaving of its individuals.

Class: Amphiprion - A More critical Glance at Ole's Family members

Inside the family Pomacentridae, Ole's process go on at the sort level, where it is ordered under Amphiprion. This sort is eminent for its relationship with ocean anemones, a one of a kind harmonious relationship that characterizes clownfish conduct. Ole imparts this trademark to different individuals from the Amphiprion sort, denoting a critical part of its ordered personality.

Species: Ole - Disclosing the Novel Character

At the zenith of Ole's logical grouping is its species name, Ole. This particular sobriquet recognizes Ole from different species inside the Amphiprion family. While Ole imparts specific qualities to its direct relations, its novel mix of hereditary characteristics, tinge, and conduct subtleties lays out it as an unmistakable animal categories, an unlikely treasure in the realm of clownfish.

Assortments and Subspecies: Unwinding Ordered Subtleties

Inside the species Ole, taxonomists might recognize assortments or subspecies in light of unpretentious varieties in variety, design, or geographic dispersion. These nuanced orders add to a more refined comprehension of Ole's variety. While the characterization of assortments or subspecies might be a subject of progressing research, it adds layers of intricacy to Ole's ordered profile.

The Job of Sub-atomic Science: Hereditary Signs in Scientific classification

Headways in sub-atomic science have upset the field of scientific categorization, giving hereditary signs that guide the order of living beings. DNA examination has turned into an incredible asset in unraveling the connections between species, genera, and families. On account of Ole, atomic methods permit researchers to investigate the hereditary subtleties that support its ordered personality, offering experiences into its developmental history and relatedness to other clownfish species.

Geographic Dissemination: An Ordered Focal point on Living space

Ole's ordered character isn't restricted to lab examinations alone; it reaches out into the immense seas where geographic dissemination turns into a significant part of its grouping. The districts where Ole is found, from the coral reefs of the Indo-Pacific to explicit pockets of the Incomparable Boundary Reef, add to how we might interpret its biological inclinations. Scientific classification, in this specific situation, fills in as a focal point through which we view Ole's territory and its transformation to different conditions.

Conduct Attributes: Ordered Experiences into Clownfish Nature

Conduct qualities, complicatedly woven into Ole's ordered texture, offer important experiences into its environmental job and connections inside the submerged local area. The exceptional ways of behaving related with Ole, whether connected with its collaboration with ocean anemones or its social elements with other clownfish, add to a comprehensive comprehension of its ordered setting. Social subtleties give taxonomists extra rules for grouping and add profundity to Ole's personality.

Scientific classification and Preservation: A Call to Protect Ole's Specialty

Understanding Ole's logical grouping is definitely not a simple practice in order; it holds significant ramifications for preservation. Ole's position in the ordered progressive system furnishes protectionists with critical data about its natural specialty, favored territories, and expected weaknesses. Saving Ole's environment becomes a question of biological stewardship as well as a method for shielding the perplexing strings of biodiversity woven into its ordered character.

Future Wildernesses: Scientific classification in the Genomic Time

The order of Ole, while enlightening its over a significant time span, likewise entices toward what's to come. As innovation keeps on propelling, the field of scientific categorization enters the genomic time, where entire genome sequencing and high level atomic strategies vow to refine how we might interpret transformative connections. The unfurling sections of scientific categorization hold the commitment of divulging new species, explaining existing groupings, and extending our appreciation for the unlikely treasures like Ole that improve the marine world.

1.2 Evolutionary History and Relationships with Other Clownfish

The transformative history of clownfish, including the less popular jewel Ole, is an enamoring story that traverses a long period of time, winding through the intricate flows of biological changes and variation. In this thorough investigation, we dig into the developmental odyssey of clownfish, following the strings that associate Ole to its precursors and disentangling the multifaceted associations with different individuals from the clownfish family.

The Old Oceans: Underlying foundations of the Clownfish Heredity

The excursion of clownfish starts in the old oceans, where the earliest precursors of this momentous family explored a world boundlessly not the same as the one we know today. Fossil records offer looks into the ancient types of clownfish, uncovering a heredity that stretches back huge number of years. These early trailblazers of the maritime domain established the groundwork for the assorted cluster of clownfish species we experience today.

Transformation and Expansion: Exploring Changing Conditions

As the seas went through extraordinary movements throughout land time scales, clownfish adjusted and expanded in light of evolving conditions. The capacity to adjust to fluctuating circumstances, from changes in ocean levels to shifts in temperature and environment accessibility, added to the transformative progress of the clownfish genealogy. Ole, similar to its precursors, conveys the hereditary tradition of transformation, a demonstration of the flexibility of this surprising family.

Normal Family: Hereditary Marks that Tight spot

Hereditary examinations give an amazing asset to disentangling the normal parentage that ties clownfish species. By contrasting DNA groupings, researchers can follow the developmental connections among Ole and other clownfish. These hereditary marks offer experiences into the fanning focuses in the transformative tree, featuring shared family line and uniqueness over the long run. Ole's hereditary cosmetics turns into a gold mine of data, uncovering its position in the more extensive clownfish family.

The Amphiprion Family: Shared Attributes and Extraordinary Personalities

Inside the transformative history of clownfish, the class Amphiprion arises as a key member, enveloping a different cluster of animal types, including Ole. Shared qualities, for example, the harmonious relationship with ocean anemones and unmistakable hue designs, join the individuals from the Amphiprion variety. However, inside this common system, every species, including Ole, brags an extraordinary set qualities that characterizes its personality inside the transformative embroidery.

Beneficial interaction with Anemones: A Key to Clownfish Achievement

One of the characterizing elements of clownfish developmental history is the advantageous connection with ocean anemones. This striking transformation, probable created more than large number of years, furnishes clownfish with security from hunters and an essential base for sending off their introductions to the encompassing waters. Ole's association with this harmonious way of life is a demonstration of the persevering through outcome of this developmental procedure inside the clownfish heredity.

Regional Way of behaving and Social Design: Examples from the Predecessors

The transformative history of clownfish is set apart by the improvement of complicated social designs and regional way of behaving. The progenitors of Ole probably participated in mind boggling moves of correspondence and progressive system, ways of behaving that keep on molding the social elements of clownfish networks today. Understanding these developmental roots gives important bits of knowledge into the versatile benefits gave by territoriality and agreeable living.

Versatile Radiation: The Assorted Group of Clownfish

The transformative history of clownfish is an account of versatile radiation, a peculiarity where a solitary precursor leads to a different exhibit of animal types, each involving a special biological specialty. Ole, as an individual from this different family, features the progress of versatile radiation inside the clownfish genealogy. From the shallow reefs to more profound waters, from dynamic hue to unobtrusive shades, the clownfish family has transmitted into a large number of structures, each finely tuned to its particular climate.

Geographic Segregation: The Impetus for Variety

Geographic segregation assumes a crucial part in the developmental history of clownfish. As populaces become isolated by topographical hindrances, for example, sea flows or changes in ocean levels, particular developmental directions unfurl. The changed types of clownfish, including Ole, owe their reality to these geological subtleties, each adjusting to the exceptional difficulties and open doors introduced by their segregated territories.

Hybridization: Intersection of Transformative Ways

In the complex dance of development, clownfish, including Ole, sporadically take part in hybridization. At the point when various species interbreed, new hereditary mixes arise, making people with a mosaic of characteristics acquired from their parent species. Hybridization fills in as a junction of developmental ways, adding to the hereditary variety inside the clownfish family. It additionally suggests charming conversation starters about the limits of species and the ease of hereditary trade in the submerged world.

Biological Specialties and Versatile Systems: Illustrations from Ole

Ole, as a less popular types of clownfish, offers a contextual investigation in the development of natural specialties and versatile methodologies. By looking at its extraordinary qualities, natural surroundings inclinations, and conduct characteristics, researchers gain experiences into the versatile systems that have permitted Ole to cut out its specialty inside the complicated trap of marine life. Ole's story turns into a microcosm of the more extensive transformative powers forming the clownfish heredity.

Transformative Tensions: Difficulties and Open doors

The transformative history of clownfish is set apart by a unique exchange of difficulties and valuable open doors. Changing natural circumstances, predation tensions, and contest for assets have driven the variation and enhancement of clownfish species over ages.

Ole, in its developmental excursion, has confronted and explored these tensions, adding to the continuous story of transformation and endurance inside the submerged domain.

Human Effect: Forming the Transformative Scene

In the cutting edge period, the developmental history of clownfish faces exceptional difficulties as human exercises influence marine biological systems. Environmental change, natural surroundings obliteration, and overfishing present new transformative tensions on clownfish populaces, including Ole. Understanding the crossing point of human effect and transformative elements is urgent for creating preservation systems that save the hereditary variety and versatile capability of clownfish species.

Protection Suggestions: Shielding the Familial Legacy

The transformative history of clownfish, with Ole as a delegate player, holds significant ramifications for preservation. Protecting the genealogical legacy of clownfish requires a complex methodology that tends to the biological strength of their territories, mitigates human-prompted dangers, and encourages a more profound comprehension of the interconnectedness of species inside the clownfish family. Ole's interesting commitment to the transformative embroidered artwork highlights the significance of shielding its hereditary heritage for people in the future.

The Fate of Clownfish Advancement: Unfamiliar Waters

As we unwind the developmental history of clownfish, including the unexpected, yet invaluable treasure Ole, we stand near the very edge of strange waters. The future of clownfish development holds secrets yet to be divulged, with continuous examination, mechanical headways, and a more profound comprehension of marine biological systems promising new experiences into the versatile directions of these striking species. Ole, as a delegate of the clownfish heredity, turns into a reference point directing us toward a more complete comprehension of the transformative powers shaping life underneath the waves.

1.3 Geographic Distribution of Ole

The geographic conveyance of Ole, a less popular types of clownfish, unfurls as a rich story of biological inclinations, natural surroundings complexities, and the sensitive dance between marine life and the huge span of the world's seas. In this thorough investigation, we set out on an excursion to diagram the confounding waters that comprise Ole's living space, looking at the key factors that impact its dispersion and revealing insight into the protection suggestions that emerge from grasping the geographic scope of this enamoring species.

Prologue to Ole's Geographic Space

Ole's geographic circulation fills in as a geographic impression, a special mark scratched upon the material of coral reefs and tropical waters. As we dig into the profundities of Ole's territory, we open the mysteries of its favored surroundings, the elements forming its dispersion, and the interconnected associations with the different biological systems it calls home.

The Coral Domains: Ole's Favored Reef Conditions

Clownfish, including Ole, are prestigious for their relationship with coral reefs. Ole's geographic circulation is unpredictably connected to the presence of sound coral biological systems, where it tracks down both shelter and food. From the lively coral nurseries of the Indo-Pacific to the rambling reefs of the Incomparable Obstruction Reef, Ole's presence is woven into the embroidery of these submerged domains.

The Indo-Pacific district stands apart as an essential field for Ole's geographic dissemination. This tremendous field envelops the rich biodiversity of the Indian Sea and the western and focal Pacific Sea. Ole's natural surroundings traverses across assorted nations, from Indonesia and Australia to the Philippines and Papua New Guinea, mirroring the geographic breadth of its favored reef conditions.

Microhabitats inside Cosmoses: Specialty Inclinations of Ole

Inside Ole's more extensive geographic conveyance, microhabitats assume a critical part in forming its confined inclinations. Ole exhibits selectivity for explicit little hiding spots inside the coral reefs, displaying a liking for shielded spaces that offer security and reasonable circumstances for settling and rearing. Understanding these microhabitat inclinations gives a nuanced viewpoint on Ole's environmental necessities.

Ocean anemones, known for their advantageous associations with clownfish, arise as key parts of Ole's microhabitat inclinations. These captivating designs act as defensive sanctuaries as well as add to the supplement trade that describes the clownfish-anemone organization. Ole's geographic circulation is, subsequently, complicatedly connected to the accessibility and variety of ocean anemones inside its picked natural surroundings.

Variations to Profundity: Ole in Shallow and Profound Waters

Ole's geographic circulation traverses a scope of profundities inside its favored reef conditions. While it frequently lives in shallow waters, where the sun's beams enter the unmistakable sea surface, Ole is additionally known to investigate further domains. The variables affecting Ole's variation to fluctuating profundities incorporate admittance to food sources, conceptive methodologies, and assurance from expected hunters.

In the shallower bits of its geographic reach, Ole takes part in ways of behaving like taking care of, social cooperations, and settling in the defensive hug of coral developments. As we adventure into more profound waters, Ole's dispersion turns into a concentrate in the adaptability and flexibility of clownfish species, unwinding the natural elements that shape their presence across various profundities.

Worldwide Areas of interest: Ole's Presence in Famous Marine Stores

Ole's geographic dissemination meets with a portion of the world's most notorious marine stores and biodiversity areas of interest. The Incomparable Boundary Reef, an UNESCO World Legacy Site, remains as a zenith in Ole's territory, displaying the complicated connections among clownfish and the different cluster of marine life inside this universally critical biological system. Investigating Ole's presence in these areas of interest gives experiences into the environmental interconnectedness that characterizes its geographic reach.

Marine stores, portrayed by severe preservation gauges and safeguarded status, assume a critical part in defending Ole's territory. As we look at Ole's geographic dispersion in these stores, we gain a more profound comprehension of the job of preservation drives in safeguarding the sensitive equilibrium of environments and guaranteeing the life span of clownfish species.

Maritime Flows and Network: Effects on Conveyance Examples

The geographic circulation of Ole isn't static; it is affected by the unique powers of maritime flows and availability. Understanding these elements unwinds the multi-faceted pathways that interface Ole's territories across tremendous stretches of sea. Sea flows act as nature's expressways, working with the dispersal of clownfish hatchlings and impacting the examples of quality stream inside populaces.

Ole's geographic dissemination is molded by the dispersal of larval clownfish, a stage in their life cycle where little, planktonic posterity leave on maritime excursions prior to subsiding into their grown-up natural surroundings. The network between various reef frameworks, driven by maritime flows, adds to the hereditary variety and strength of Ole populaces, uncovering the significance of keeping up with solid halls for larval dispersal.

Environment and Temperature: Impacts on Ole's Natural surroundings Reach

Environment and temperature assume critical parts in molding the geographic dissemination of marine species, including Ole. As environmental change achieves shifts in sea temperature and ocean level, Ole's living space range faces dynamic difficulties. Understanding the connection among Ole and climatic variables gives fundamental bits of knowledge into the species' weakness and strength despite ecological changes.

Hotter waters, affected by environment examples like El Niño occasions, can influence the wellbeing of coral reefs and the accessibility of appropriate living spaces for Ole. Changes in ocean surface temperatures may likewise impact the planning of conceptive occasions and larval turn of events. Ole's geographic dispersion turns into an indicator for the more extensive effects of environmental change on marine biological systems, underscoring the earnestness of protection measures to moderate these impacts.

Endemism and Biodiversity: Ole's Commitment to Nearby Environments

Ole's geographic circulation isn't uniform across all districts; it adds to the rich embroidery of endemism and biodiversity inside unambiguous areas. The presence of Ole in specific regions might be demonstrative of exceptional biological circumstances, adding to the general biodiversity of clownfish species in those areas. Investigating the examples of endemism inside Ole's geographic reach divulges the perplexing connections among species and their territories.

Limited endemism, where Ole is tracked down solely inside unambiguous districts, features the meaning of saving these regions for the preservation of one of a kind hereditary qualities and natural elements. The investigation of Ole's geographic circulation turns into a critical part in distinguishing areas of high biodiversity and focusing on preservation endeavors to safeguard the sensitive equilibrium of marine environments.

Preservation Areas of interest: Ole's Geographic Reach needing Assurance

The acknowledgment of Ole's geographic dissemination as a protection area of interest highlights the criticalness of shielding its environment. Protection areas of interest are locales described by elevated degrees of biodiversity and biological importance, putting forth them central focuses for preservation attempts. Ole's presence inside these areas of interest flags the requirement for designated protection systems to address expected dangers and guarantee the drawn out endurance of this less popular clownfish species.

Human exercises, including overfishing, natural surroundings obliteration, and contamination, present critical dangers to Ole's geographic appropriation. Preservation drives should address these difficulties, advancing reasonable practices and local area association to safeguard the natural surroundings that Ole and other marine species rely upon. Ole's commitment to the more extensive marine biological system turns into a mobilizing point for traditionalists pushing for the protection of the world's seas.

Examination and Checking: Divulging the Secrets of Ole's Living space

The geographic appropriation of Ole stays a continuous subject of exploration and checking. Researchers utilize a scope of strategies, from submerged studies to satellite symbolism and hereditary examinations, to disentangle the secrets of Ole's territory.

The nonstop observing of Ole's geographic reach gives fundamental information to understanding populace elements, distinguishing shifts in circulation examples, and illuminating preservation methodologies.

Research drives dive into the microhabitats, regenerative ways of behaving, and environmental collaborations inside Ole's geographic conveyance. Satellite following innovation permits researchers to investigate the developments of clownfish populaces, revealing insight into the variables impacting their dispersal and availability between various reef frameworks. These exploration tries add to a thorough comprehension of Ole's environment prerequisites and help in the improvement of compelling protection measures.

Local area Commitment: Enabling Neighborhood Stewardship

Protecting Ole's geographic dispersion requires a cooperative methodology that connects with nearby networks in stewardship and preservation endeavors. Local area based drives, for example, marine safeguarded regions and manageable the travel industry rehearses, assume a significant part in protecting Ole's living space. By engaging neighborhood networks as caretakers of their marine surroundings, moderates cultivate a feeling of obligation for the drawn out wellbeing of Ole's geographic reach.

Instructive projects, outreach drives, and organizations with neighborhood partners add to building mindfulness about Ole and its biological importance. As people group become effectively engaged with the protection of Ole's living space, the far reaching influences stretch out past geographic limits, making an organization of marine stewards focused on the prosperity of clownfish species and their biological systems.

The Job of Aquariums: Protection Through Hostage Reproducing

Aquariums and marine examination establishments add to the safeguarding of Ole's geographic appropriation through hostage reproducing programs. These drives, directed in controlled conditions, assist with mitigating the tension on wild populaces while giving significant bits of knowledge into the conceptive science and conduct of clownfish species. The effective rearing of Ole in aquariums fills in as a protection device, offering a possible life saver for the species.

Hostage rearing projects additionally add to public mindfulness and schooling about Ole and its living space. Aquariums act as instructive center points, encouraging an association among guests and the submerged world. By exhibiting Ole in controlled conditions, aquariums add to logical information as well as move a feeling of marvel and appreciation for the magnificence and delicacy of Ole's geographic dissemination.

Worldwide Cooperation: A Worldwide Work to Safeguard Ole's Natural surroundings

Safeguarding Ole's geographic conveyance requires worldwide cooperation and a common obligation to marine protection. Associations, specialists, and state run administrations from various nations contribute their aptitude and assets to screen and safeguard Ole and its territory. The sharing of information, best practices, and preservation procedures cultivates an aggregate work to address the complicated difficulties confronting Ole's geographic reach.

Peaceful accords and shows, like the Show on Organic Variety and the Unified Countries Supportable Improvement Objectives, give systems to worldwide participation in marine preservation. By perceiving the interconnectedness of marine biological systems and the significance of Ole's geographic appropriation, the global local area moves toward guaranteeing the strength and maintainability of the world's seas.

Chapter 2

Physical Characteristics

The actual qualities of Ole, a less popular types of clownfish, comprise a hypnotizing embroidery of varieties, designs, and unmistakable highlights that put it aside inside the perplexing universe of marine life. In this investigation, we dive into the profundities of Ole's actual properties, disentangling the mysteries of its appearance, conduct, and variations that add to its one of a kind personality.

Particular Hue: Nature's Range in Ole's Scales

At the core of Ole's actual qualities lies its unmistakable shading, a show-stopper created naturally's range. Ole, in the same way as other clownfish species, shows lively tints of orange, yellow, and white, making a striking differentiation against the background of coral reefs. The distinctive varieties fill different needs, from drawing in mates to laying an out area and imparting inside the social pecking order of clownfish networks.

Ole's shading goes through inconspicuous changes all through its life, with adolescents frequently showing various examples and tints contrasted with grown-ups. These progressions are stylishly enamoring as well as assume urgent parts in flagging physiological states and social elements inside Ole's territory. The development of these shading designs divulges a unique exchange between hereditary qualities, natural elements, and the versatile procedures utilized by Ole all through its life.

Stripes and Examples: Nature's Disguise for Ole

Notwithstanding its base hue, Ole is embellished with unmistakable stripes and examples that act as nature's cover in the submerged world. The course of action of groups across Ole's body shifts among people and species, adding to their capacity to mix flawlessly into the coral conditions they possess. These examples give a visual display for spectators as well as fundamental instruments for Ole's endurance.

The stripes on Ole's body add to its capacity to explore and disguise inside the perplexing designs of coral reefs. The many-sided equilibrium of light and shadow in these conditions is reflected in Ole's stripes, permitting it to explore securely and stow away from expected hunters. The development of these examples mirrors the versatile systems sharpened by Ole over ages, a demonstration of the complicated dance among structure and capability in the submerged domain.

Morphological Subtleties: From Blades to Anemone-Adjusted Bodies

Ole's actual qualities reach out past hue to envelop a scope of morphological subtleties that characterize its novel personality inside the clownfish family. From the effortless range of blades to the specific variations work with its harmonious relationship with ocean anemones, Ole's morphology mirrors a finely tuned blend of structure and capability.

The pectoral balances of Ole, sensitive and extended, add to its agile developments inside the water. These blades are apparatuses for impetus as well as fundamental for keeping up with equilibrium and mobility, qualities critical for Ole's endurance in the complex and dynamic climate of coral reefs. The advancement of these balances addresses the particular tensions applied by the submerged world, molding Ole's morphology throughout transformative time.

Ole's body is likewise adjusted for its cooperative relationship with ocean anemones, a central trait of clownfish species. Not at all like other fish that keep away from the stinging limbs of anemones, Ole has a defensive layer of bodily fluid on skin forestalls the nematocysts (stinging cells) of the anemone from hurting it. This transformation permits Ole to look for shelter and lay out a commonly valuable relationship with ocean anemones, giving security in return to food.

The mouth of Ole is interestingly adjusted for benefiting from a shifted diet that incorporates little spineless creatures and zooplankton. The terminal mouth, situated toward the finish of the nose, considers accuracy in catching prey inside the perplexing designs of coral reefs. This transformation adds to Ole's flexibility as a forager, empowering it to take advantage of the rich assets accessible in its environment.

Size and Sexual Dimorphism: Fluctuated Heights in Ole's People group

Ole, in the same way as other clownfish species, displays sexual dimorphism in size, where guys and females contrast in height. This size contrast is especially articulated in some clownfish species, with females for the most part being bigger than guys. Understanding the sexual dimorphism in size adds to bits of knowledge into the conceptive methodologies and social elements inside Ole's people group.

In some clownfish species, including possibly Ole, the biggest person in a gathering is a female, while the following biggest is a physically full grown male. The excess individuals from the gathering are more modest, non-regenerative guys. The progressive design inside Ole's people group, in light of size and regenerative jobs, assumes an essential part in keeping social control and adding to the general wellness of the gathering.

The size variety inside Ole's people group likewise stretches out to the singular development directions of clownfish. Factors like sustenance, social communications, and ecological circumstances can impact the development paces of people. Understanding the examples of size variety adds as far as anyone is concerned of the variables forming the socioeconomics and elements of Ole's populaces inside unambiguous environments.

Social Attributes: Articulations of Ole's Actual Character

Ole's actual qualities are not static; they show some major signs of life through a horde of social characteristics that express its personality inside the perplexing dance of clownfish networks. From regional showcases to romance customs, Ole's ways of behaving offer windows into its social elements, correspondence methodologies, and versatile reactions to the difficulties of its natural surroundings.

Territoriality is an unmistakable social characteristic among clownfish, including Ole. The foundation and guard of domains inside the coral reef fill numerous needs, from giving a place of refuge to taking care of and settling to flagging regenerative wellness to possible mates. Ole's regional ways of behaving are communicated through visual presentations, including balance developments and body stances, as well as through vocalizations that impart its presence and status to other clownfish.

Romance ceremonies unfurl as a feature of Ole's regenerative ways of behaving, where the energetic hue and multifaceted developments become vital parts of the mating dance. Male clownfish, including Ole, put critical exertion in seeking females, exhibiting their hereditary wellness and appropriateness as mates. The romance ceremonies of Ole contribute not exclusively to effective generation yet additionally to the foundation of social securities inside the clownfish local area.

Correspondence inside Ole's people group is an intricate interaction of visual and substance signals. The variety changes, balance developments, and body stances saw in Ole pass on messages about friendly progressive system, conceptive availability, and regional limits. Substance signs, delivered through the bodily fluid on Ole's skin, assume a part in laying out acknowledgment among individuals from its local arca, adding to the union and collaboration inside the gathering.

Advantageous Connections: Ole and Ocean Anemones as one

One of the most intriguing parts of Ole's actual attributes is its harmonious relationship with ocean anemones. This extraordinary affiliation is a characterizing element of clownfish species, where Ole tracks down shelter and insurance inside the stinging limbs of ocean anemones, while furnishing the anemones with food and supplements.

Ole's actual qualities are unpredictably connected to its capacity to flourish inside the antagonistic climate of ocean anemones. The defensive layer of bodily fluid on Ole's skin forestalls the nematocysts of the anemone from stinging, permitting Ole to explore and look for cover inside the appendages. The tinge and examples of Ole likewise add to its cover inside the anemone, giving an extra layer of security from expected hunters.

The harmonious connection among Ole and ocean anemones isn't only a latent affiliation; it includes dynamic correspondence and collaboration. Ole takes part in ways of behaving, for example, "moving" inside the limbs of the anemone, a cycle that adjusts the anemone to its presence and lays out a commonly gainful compatibility.

The transformation of Ole's actual qualities to this advantageous way of life represents the mind boggling relationship that portrays marine environments.

Regenerative Procedures: Sustaining the Future

Ole's actual qualities assume a vital part in its regenerative procedures, which are finely tuned to guarantee the endurance and outcome of the future. Clownfish, including Ole, are known for their remarkable regenerative ways of behaving, where a gathering involves a prevailing rearing pair and non-conceptive people. Understanding the regenerative procedures of Ole gives bits of knowledge into the complicated elements of clownfish networks.

The female Ole, for the most part bigger than the male, expects the job of the prevailing reproducing individual inside the gathering. The various leveled structure, in view of size and conceptive jobs, is kept up with through conduct connections and correspondence signals. The male, frequently the second-biggest individual, helps the female in home readiness and shields the domain against likely dangers.

The settling conduct of Ole includes the readiness and support of a settling site, frequently a level surface inside the coral reef. The female stores her eggs on this substrate, and the male treats them remotely. The male then, at that point, expects the job of gatekeeper, industriously shielding the eggs from possible hunters and guaranteeing their prosperity until they hatch into hatchlings.

The advancement of Ole's regenerative procedures mirrors the particular tensions of its natural surroundings, where the accessibility of reasonable settling destinations, the presence of hunters, and the elements of the gathering impact the outcome of propagation. Ole's actual attributes, from its size and hue to its ways of behaving and variations, add to the complicated trap of conceptive procedures that characterize clownfish networks.

Ecological Impacts: Adjusting to Changing Circumstances

Ole's actual attributes are formed by its hereditary cosmetics as well as by the impacts of its current circumstance. The unique idea of coral reef biological systems, affected by variables like water temperature, supplement accessibility, and the soundness of the coral territory, can influence the declaration of Ole's actual characteristics and ways of behaving.

Temperature, for example, assumes an essential part in molding the tinge examples of Ole. Changes in water temperature can impact the dissemination of shades inside the skin cells of clownfish, prompting varieties in variety power and example. Observing these varieties furnishes researchers with bits of knowledge into the possible effects of environmental change on the actual attributes of Ole and other clownfish species.

The soundness of coral reefs, Ole's essential natural surroundings, likewise impacts its actual qualities. Coral fading, a peculiarity connected to increasing ocean temperatures, can influence the accessibility of reasonable settling locales and the overflow of prey inside Ole's current circumstance. Understanding the connections between Ole's actual characteristics and ecological impacts is fundamental for anticipating and moderating the likely impacts of living space debasement on clownfish populaces.

Preservation Suggestions: Shielding Ole's Actual Variety

The actual qualities of Ole hold significant ramifications for its protection, as they are unpredictably connected to its capacity to flourish inside unambiguous natural specialties. Saving Ole's actual variety requires a comprehensive methodology that tends to the interconnected elements impacting its appearance, ways of behaving, and variations.

Living space preservation remains as a foundation of endeavors to shield Ole's actual qualities. Safeguarding the wellbeing and strength of coral reef biological systems guarantees the accessibility of reasonable territories, settling locales, and prey assets for Ole and other clownfish species. Marine safeguarded regions, feasible fishing practices, and measures to relieve the effects of environmental change add to the conservation of Ole's natural surroundings.

Local area commitment and training assume significant parts in advancing the preservation of Ole's actual variety. By bringing issues to light about the special qualities and biological significance of clownfish, including Ole, progressives engage neighborhood networks to become advocates for marine stewardship. Understanding the sensitive harmony between Ole's actual qualities and its current circumstance encourages a feeling of obligation for the prosperity of this unlikely treasure inside the submerged world.

Research drives zeroed in on Ole's actual attributes add as far as anyone is concerned of the species and illuminate preservation methodologies. Observing changes in hue designs, concentrating on ways of behaving, and investigating the versatile reactions of Ole to natural difficulties give fundamental information to traditionalists endeavoring to safeguard this less popular clownfish species.

Worldwide cooperation is principal for the protection of Ole's actual variety. Given Ole's geographic conveyance across various districts and the interconnectedness of marine environments, a worldwide exertion is expected to address the complicated difficulties confronting clownfish populaces. Shared research tries, protection drives, and strategy measures add to an aggregate obligation to shielding Ole and safeguarding the actual variety that improves the submerged domain.

2.1 Distinctive Coloration and Patterns

The particular shading and examples of Ole, a less popular types of clownfish, unfurl as an enthralling visual ensemble underneath the waves, adding to its exceptional character inside the different embroidery of marine life. In this investigation, we jump into the complexities of Ole's shading and examples, unwinding the transformative importance, utilitarian variations, and stylish wonders that characterize this unlikely treasure of the reef.

The Lively Range of Ole's Tones

At the core of Ole's visual charm lies a lively range of tones that dance across its scales. The essential shades of orange, yellow, and white mix flawlessly, making an amicable organization that contrasts the scenery of coral reefs. The development of these shades fills a huge number of needs, from correspondence inside clownfish networks to the foundation of regions and romance customs.

Ole's orange tinge, specifically, is a sign of numerous clownfish species. The distinctive orange tone enraptures onlookers as well as assumes a significant part in flagging regenerative wellness. In the submerged existence where light is specifically sifted, the splendor of Ole's orange variety sticks out, considering powerful correspondence and acknowledgment among people inside its local area.

The shades of yellow and white that embellish Ole's body add to its general disguise inside the coral reef climate. The multifaceted examples and varieties in variety thickness assist Ole with mixing consistently with the coral developments, giving a degree of security from likely hunters. The mix of these shades exhibits the fragile harmony between the requirement for perceivability inside the local area and the basic to stay hid inside the complicated designs of the reef.

Developmental Importance: Nature's Brushstrokes on Ole's Material

The development of Ole's particular hue and examples is a demonstration of the mind boggling dance between specific tensions and versatile procedures that have molded clownfish species more than great many years. In the huge spread of the sea, where hunters and prey explore a universe of moving light and shadow, Ole's tinge turns into a device for correspondence, cover, and species acknowledgment.

The developmental meaning of Ole's tinge is intently attached to its harmonious relationship with ocean anemones. The dynamic tints of Ole not just act as visual signs inside its local area yet additionally add to the foundation and support of the one of a kind organization with ocean anemones. The many-sided dance of advancement has tweaked Ole's tinge to line up with the requirements of its way of life and biological specialty.

The course of regular determination has leaned toward variety designs that improve Ole's endurance inside unambiguous environments. Examples of stripes, bars, and varieties in variety power are not erratic; they are the consequence of a perplexing exchange between hereditary characteristics, ecological impacts, and the requirement for viable correspondence and security. The brushstrokes of development have painted Ole's material with a range of varieties that addresses its flexibility and variation inside the unique submerged domain.

Utilitarian Variations: Stripes, Bars, and Disguise Dominance

The particular examples that enhance Ole's body are not only tasteful; they serve utilitarian transformations that add to its endurance and accomplishment inside the coral reef environment. Stripes and bars, organized in special arrangements, are key components of Ole's visual language, working with correspondence, social elements, and route inside the complicated designs of the reef.

1. **Social Flagging: Stripes as a Specialized Instrument**
   Ole's stripes assume a significant part in friendly motioning inside its local area. Clownfish, including Ole, are known for their progressive social designs, where

prevailing people lay out domains and romance ceremonies. The game plan and power of stripes pass on data about a singular's status, conceptive preparation, and regional limits.

Prevailing people frequently show more articulated and clear cut stripes, flagging their situation inside the social order. Subordinate people might show varieties in stripe power, mirroring their status inside the gathering. The utilization of stripes as a visual language inside Ole's people group is a dynamic and steadily changing articulation of social communications and connections.

2. **Disguise Dominance: Examples for Covering**

The perplexing examples of Ole's tinge act as a breathtaking type of cover inside the coral reef climate. The exchanging groups of variety, frequently organized such that imitates the encompassing coral developments, empower Ole to mix consistently into its living space. This disguise isn't static; it adjusts to various microhabitats and lighting conditions, giving Ole a flexible device for camouflage.

The adequacy of Ole's cover is elevated by its capacity to specifically change its tinge in view of its environmental factors. This versatile component permits Ole to explore the perplexing designs of the coral reef without causing excessive to notice itself. The development of these cover techniques mirrors the consistent interchange between predation pressures and the requirement for Ole to stay unnoticeable inside its current circumstance.

3. **Romance Ceremonies: Examples as a Visual Orchestra**

Ole's tinge and examples become the overwhelming focus during romance ceremonies, changing into a visual orchestra that imparts regenerative preparation and hereditary wellness. Male clownfish, including Ole, put huge exertion in exhibiting their energetic varieties and mind boggling examples to draw in possible mates.

The romance dance of Ole includes the showcase of uplifted variety force, many-sided blade developments, and exact body stances. The examples on Ole's body become a material for communicating hereditary imperativeness, and females are attracted to guys with the most energetic and clear cut markings. The romance customs add to effective generation as well as feature the tasteful and practical elements of Ole's shading inside the setting of species endurance.

Versatile Reactions: Variety Changes and Natural Elements

The versatile reactions of Ole's hue reach out past static examples, including dynamic changes that mirror its capacity to answer natural signs and physiological states. The variety changes saw in Ole are not just articulations of social signs and romance shows yet additionally reactions to elements like pressure, ecological circumstances, and conceptive status.

1. **Stress-Instigated Variety Changes: A Window into Ole's Prosperity**
   Clownfish, including Ole, show pressure prompted variety changes as a reaction to outside improvements or unsettling influences in their current circumstance. Stressors like the presence of possible hunters, changes in water quality, or disturbances inside the gathering can set off shifts in Ole's hue. These progressions act as visual signs of Ole's prosperity and the need to adjust to evolving conditions.

   Stress-prompted variety changes in Ole might appear as an obscuring or easing up of its general shading. Understanding these reactions gives significant bits of knowledge into the elements affecting Ole's physiological state and the possible effects of ecological aggravations on its wellbeing. Preservation endeavors pointed toward limiting stressors add to the general prosperity of Ole populaces inside their environments.

2. **Ecological Impacts: Variety and Environment Elements**

The shading of Ole is impacted by natural elements, remembering varieties for water temperature and light circumstances. Changes in these natural boundaries can affect the circulation of shades inside Ole's skin cells, prompting varieties in variety force and example. Observing these variety varieties furnishes researchers with important information on the impacts of environment elements on Ole's physiology and conduct.

Hotter water temperatures, affected by environment examples like El Niño occasions, may impact the hue of Ole and other clownfish species. The versatile reactions of Ole to these varieties highlight its strength and ability to conform to changing ecological circumstances. Concentrating on these reactions adds to how we might interpret the more extensive effects of environmental change on marine species and biological systems.

Protection Suggestions: Saving Ole's Visual Quality
The particular shading and examples of Ole hold significant ramifications for its protection, as they are indispensable parts of its versatile procedures and biological cooperations inside coral reef environments. Saving Ole's visual magnificence requires a complete methodology that tends to the interconnected variables impacting its shading, examples, and reactions to natural elements.

1. **Territory Preservation: Safeguarding the Material of Coral Reefs**
   The essential material whereupon Ole's shading and examples become completely awake is the coral reef natural surroundings. Environment protection remains as a foundation of endeavors to shield Ole's visual wonder. Marine safeguarded regions, supportable fishing practices, and measures to alleviate the effects of environmental change add to the conservation of the assorted and complex conditions that Ole and other clownfish species call home.

Safeguarding the wellbeing and strength of coral reefs guarantees not just the accessibility of reasonable living spaces for Ole yet additionally the wealth of prey assets and microhabitats fundamental for its endurance. Protection drives that attention on keeping up with the honesty of coral reef environments add to the visual ensemble of varieties that describe Ole's submerged world.

2. **Examination and Checking: Disclosing the Elements of Hue**

   Research drives zeroed in on Ole's tinge and examples add as far as anyone is concerned of the species and illuminate preservation methodologies. Checking changes in shading designs gives fundamental information to figuring out the physiological reactions of Ole to natural changes, stressors, and aggravations.

   Logical exploration additionally investigates the likely effects of environmental change on Ole's shading, revealing insight into the versatile limit of clownfish species inside the setting of more extensive natural movements. The nonstop observing of Ole's visual wonder fills in as a gauge for the general wellbeing and strength of coral reef biological systems, directing preservation endeavors toward proof based methodologies.

3. **Local area Commitment: Cultivating Appreciation and Stewardship**

   Protecting Ole's visual magnificence requires the dynamic cooperation of nearby networks and partners. Local area commitment and training assume urgent parts in cultivating appreciation for the extraordinary qualities of clownfish, including Ole, and advancing mindful stewardship of marine conditions.

   By bringing issues to light about the sensitive harmony between Ole's tinge, designs, and its environmental importance, preservationists engage neighborhood networks to become advocates for marine protection. Instructive projects, outreach drives, and organizations with nearby partners add to building an organization of marine stewards focused on the prosperity of Ole and its submerged buddies.

4. **Environment Activity: Alleviating Effects on Ole's Material**

Tending to the more extensive effects of environmental change is fundamental for the drawn out protection of Ole's visual magnificence. Environment activity estimates that plan to lessen fossil fuel byproducts, moderate the impacts of climbing ocean temperatures, and elevate reasonable practices add to the strength of coral reef biological systems.

Worldwide cooperation is urgent in the worldwide work to address environmental change and its effects on marine biodiversity. By perceiving the interconnectedness of environments and the significance of safeguarding Ole's visual magnificence, the global local area moves toward guaranteeing the life span of the world's seas and the lively varieties that portray Ole's natural surroundings.

2.2 Size and Morphological Features

The size and morphological highlights of Ole, a less popular types of clownfish, lay out a picture of variation and utilitarian variety inside the powerful universe of coral reefs. Ole displays sexual dimorphism, with females for the most part being bigger than guys. This size variety adds to the various leveled structure inside Ole's gatherings, where the biggest individual frequently accepts the job of the prevailing rearing female.

Morphologically, Ole's highlights grandstand a finely tuned mix of structure and capability. Lengthened and sensitive pectoral blades empower agile developments, fundamental for exploring the complex designs of coral reefs. The terminal mouth, situated toward the finish of the nose, reflects specific transformations for exact scavenging inside Ole's living space. Besides, Ole's capacity to frame cooperative associations with ocean anemones is highlighted by a defensive layer of bodily fluid on its skin, forestalling the nematocysts of the anemone from really hurting.

In rundown, Ole's size and morphological highlights typify the transformative reactions sharpened by clownfish species, adding to their prosperity inside the mind boggling and dynamic environments of coral reefs.

2.3 Behavioral Traits that Set Ole Apart

The conduct characteristics displayed by Ole, a less popular types of clownfish, put it aside as an interesting and particular individual from the submerged local area. These conduct subtleties not just add to the complicated social elements inside clownfish gatherings yet additionally assume a vital part in Ole's endurance and variation inside its coral reef environment.

Territoriality is a conspicuous social quality showed by Ole, as well as other clownfish species. Ole lays out and protects domains inside the coral reef, making places of refuge for taking care of, settling, and other fundamental exercises. Regional presentations include balance developments, body stances, and even vocalizations, filling in as visual and hear-able signals that impart Ole's presence and status inside the social pecking order.

Romance ceremonies unfurl as a hypnotizing dance, exhibiting Ole's dynamic hue and multifaceted developments. Male clownfish, including Ole, put huge exertion in seeking females, showing hereditary wellness and reasonableness as mates. The romance customs are not simply prefaces to generation; they add to the foundation of social securities inside the clownfish local area and support the union of the gathering.

Correspondence inside Ole's people group is a complicated interaction of visual and substance signals. The lively variety changes, blade developments, and body stances saw in Ole pass on messages about friendly progressive system, conceptive preparation, and regional limits. Synthetic prompts, delivered through the bodily fluid on Ole's skin, add to the acknowledgment and attachment of the clownfish bunch, encouraging participation and common help.

One of the most astounding parts of Ole's way of behaving is its cooperative relationship with ocean anemones. Dissimilar to other fish that keep away from the stinging limbs of anemones, Ole has a defensive layer of bodily fluid on its skin, forestalling the nematocysts from truly hurting.

Ole effectively takes part in ways of behaving, for example, "moving" inside the limbs of the anemone, adapting it to its presence and laying out a mutualistic compatibility. This harmonious affiliation gives Ole shelter and insurance, while the anemone benefits from food and supplements gave by the clownfish.

Moreover, Ole's social reactions incorporate versatile techniques to changing natural circumstances. These may remember shifts for social elements, like modifications in regional limits or changes in the social progressive system, as well as reactions to stressors or aggravations in the coral reef environment.

In rundown, the conduct characteristics that put Ole aside inside the clownfish family reveal an embroidery of social connections, correspondence systems, and versatile reactions to the difficulties of its territory. From regional presentations to romance ceremonies and cooperative associations, Ole's ways of behaving are fundamental to its personality and accomplishment inside the energetic submerged universe of coral reefs. Understanding and valuing these conduct complexities contribute not exclusively to logical information yet in addition to the more extensive account of marine biodiversity and the preservation goals of Ole and its individual clownfish species.

Chapter 3

Habitat And Ecology

The living space and biology of Ole, a less popular types of clownfish, structure an enamoring story of variation and interconnected connections inside the unique domain of coral reefs. In this investigation, we dig into the complexities of Ole's picked natural surroundings, its biological jobs, and the cooperative connections that characterize its presence in the submerged world.

1. **Territory Inclinations: Exploring the Coral Domains of the Indo-Pacific**
   Ole's natural surroundings inclinations are complicatedly connected to the coral reefs of the Indo-Pacific district, where the species tracks down its specialty in the midst of the dynamic and complex environments. These coral reefs act as the material whereupon Ole's life unfurls, exhibiting an inclination for explicit natural circumstances that add to its endurance and propagation.
   The Indo-Pacific district, eminent for its rich biodiversity and coral variety, furnishes Ole with a different exhibit of environments. Inside this huge spread, Ole is known to possess coral arrangements portrayed by stretching and even designs. The presence of appropriate settling destinations, closeness to prey assets, and the accessibility of likely harmonious accomplices, for example, ocean anemones, impact Ole's choice of living spaces.
   The multifaceted engineering of coral reefs offers Ole safe house and shelter as well as an overflow of microhabitats that take special care of its differed needs. From hole inside coral branches to the sandy substrates encompassing coral developments, Ole explores these conditions with the finesse of an animal finely sensitive to the subtleties of its picked territory.
2. **Natural Jobs: The Fragile Dance of Transformation and Commitment**
   Ole, as other clownfish species, assumes vital biological parts inside its natural surroundings, adding to the fragile equilibrium of coral reef environments. Understanding these jobs discloses the unpredictable dance of variation and commitment that characterizes Ole's spot in the submerged local area.

Regional Guardianship: Molding the Social Texture

Territoriality is a noticeable environmental pretended by Ole inside its local area. Laying out and guarding regions inside the coral reef fills different needs, from giving places of refuge to taking care of and settling to flagging conceptive wellness to expected mates.

The presence of Ole inside a region adds to the forming of social elements, where progressive designs characterize the communications and connections among clownfish people.

Regional guardianship includes visual presentations, including balance developments and body stances, as well as vocalizations that impart Ole's presence and status. The foundation of regions improves the general soundness and union of the clownfish local area, adding to its strength and versatility inside the coral reef environment.

Prey Elements: Scrounging Procedures and Dietary Inclinations

Ole's natural job stretches out to its rummaging systems and dietary inclinations, which are finely tuned to the assets accessible inside its territory. Clownfish, including Ole, are omnivorous feeders, consuming a fluctuated diet that incorporates little spineless creatures, zooplankton, and green growth.

The terminal mouth of Ole is adjusted for accuracy in catching prey inside the multifaceted designs of coral reefs. This scrounging transformation permits Ole to take advantage of the assets present in its environment effectively. The environmental cooperations among Ole and its prey add to the guideline of invertebrate populaces inside the coral reef biological system, impacting the general wellbeing and elements of the local area.

Cooperative Affiliations: Ole and Ocean Anemones as one

One of the most interesting biological jobs of Ole is its harmonious relationship with ocean anemones. Dissimilar to other fish that stay away from the stinging limbs of anemones, Ole effectively looks for shelter and insurance inside the limbs, laying out a mutualistic affiliation. This novel organization characterizes Ole's biological specialty and adds to the biodiversity and dependability of coral reef environments.

The harmonious relationship includes a sensitive dance of transformation and collaboration. Ole has a defensive layer of bodily fluid on its skin, forestalling the nematocysts (stinging cells) of the anemone from hurting. Consequently, Ole furnishes the anemone with food and supplements got from its rummaging exercises. The presence of Ole inside the anemone adds to the general wellbeing and life span of these indispensable coral reef occupants.

Regenerative Elements: Adding to Hereditary Variety

Ole's biological importance is additionally complemented by its part in the regenerative elements of clownfish networks. Inside gatherings, Ole expects conceptive jobs, with predominant females participating in settling ways of behaving and guys aiding home planning and safeguard.

The environmental commitment of Ole to conceptive elements reaches out past individual reproducing matches. The progressive construction inside Ole's people group, in light of size and regenerative jobs, impacts the hereditary variety and strength of the populace. The fruitful multiplication of Ole adds to the continuous imperativeness and flexibility of clownfish populaces inside the coral reef environment.

3. **Advantageous Connections: Ole and the Submerged Ensemble**

Ole's environment and biology are profoundly laced with its advantageous connections, especially its relationship with ocean anemones. This beneficial interaction, described by common advantages and mind boggling ways of behaving, structures a foundation of Ole's presence in the coral reef environment.

Defensive Advantageous interaction: Ole's Transformations to The ocean Anemones

The defensive beneficial interaction among Ole and ocean anemones is a surprising illustration of transformation and participation. Ole effectively looks for asylum inside the stinging arms of the anemone, using its defensive layer of bodily fluid to keep hurt from the nematocysts. This variation permits Ole to explore and dwell inside the anemone's limbs without setting off a protective reaction.The advantages of this cooperative affiliation are equal. Ole acquires security from possible hunters, using the anemone's stinging capacities as an obstruction. Consequently, Ole furnishes the anemone with food and supplements got from its scrounging exercises. The dance among Ole and the ocean anemone is an ensemble of transformation, where the two accomplices add to one another's prosperity and endurance.

Social Cooperations: Moving Inside the Limbs

The social cooperations among Ole and ocean anemones reach out past simple asylum. Ole takes part in a novel way of behaving known as "moving" inside the limbs of the anemone. This interaction includes a progression of developments and contacts that adapt the anemone to Ole's presence, keeping a forceful reaction from the stinging cells.

The moving way of behaving is an entrancing illustration of correspondence and collaboration inside harmonious connections. Ole's capacity to lay out an amicable compatibility with the ocean anemone adds to the security and life span of this crucial natural organization. The social complexities of moving inside the arms feature the versatility and knowledge of Ole in exploring its advantageous affiliations.

Taking care of and Supplement Trade: The Money of Advantageous interaction

The advantageous connection among Ole and ocean anemones includes something other than assurance. Ole effectively adds to the nourishing requirements of the anemone through taking care of exercises. As Ole searches for little spineless creatures and zooplankton, it gives a part of its discoveries to the anemone, upgrading its supplement consumption.

This taking care of and supplement trade are fundamental parts of the cooperative money among Ole and ocean anemones. The supplements got from Ole's scavenging exercises supplement the anemone's eating routine, encouraging a commonly valuable game plan. The biological ramifications of this supplement trade reach out to the general wellbeing and flexibility of the two accomplices inside the coral reef environment.

4. **Ecological Impacts: Adjusting to the Elements of Coral Reefs**

   Ole's natural surroundings and biology are dependent upon the unique impacts of the coral reef climate. The collaborations among Ole and its environmental elements are molded by natural factors that add to its versatile procedures and reactions to evolving conditions.

   Temperature and Coral Wellbeing: Effect on Ole's Prosperity

   The temperature of the coral reef climate assumes a crucial part in molding the living space and environment of Ole. Coral reefs are delicate to changes in water temperature, and variances can impact the strength of the coral settlements that give cover and settling destinations to Ole.

   Ole's prosperity is unpredictably connected to the wellbeing of coral reefs, as these designs act as the groundwork of its environment. Climbing ocean temperatures, credited to environmental change, can bring about coral fading, a peculiarity where corals remove the cooperative green growth that give them tone and supplements. The corruption of coral wellbeing presents difficulties to Ole's versatile procedures, influencing settling locales and the accessibility of prey assets.

   Water Quality and Stress Reactions: Signs of Ecological Wellbeing

   The nature of water inside the coral reef climate is a urgent element impacting Ole's way of behaving and prosperity. Changes in water quality, whether because of contamination or regular vacillations, can get pressure reactions in clownfish, including Ole. These pressure actuated reactions might appear as adjustments in hue or conduct changes, giving significant marks of the natural soundness of the reef.

   Ole's aversion to changes in water quality highlights the interconnectedness of its nature with more extensive coral reef elements. Observing pressure reactions in Ole adds to the evaluation of ecological circumstances and helps protection endeavors zeroed in on safeguarding the wellbeing and versatility of coral reefs.

5. **Preservation Suggestions: Protecting Ole's Natural surroundings and Biology**

The natural surroundings and environment of Ole convey significant ramifications for protection endeavors pointed toward safeguarding the biodiversity and biological equilibrium of coral reefs. Perceiving the interconnected connections, social complexities, and harmonious relationship of Ole adds to a comprehensive way to deal with marine protection.

Environment Protection: Saving the Coral Material

Environment protection remains as a primary mainstay of endeavors to defend Ole's living space and nature. Safeguarding the wellbeing and versatility of coral reefs guarantees the accessibility of reasonable settling destinations, microhabitats, and prey assets for Ole and other clownfish species.

Marine safeguarded regions, economical fishing practices, and drives to alleviate the effects of environmental change are pivotal parts of territory protection. By safeguarding the mind boggling material of coral reefs, preservationists add to the life span of Ole's presence and the heap life frames that depend on these biological systems.

Local area Commitment and Schooling: Backers for Marine Stewardship

Drawing in neighborhood networks and cultivating schooling are fundamental procedures in the protection of Ole's environment and biology. By bringing issues to light about the novel attributes and biological significance of clownfish, including Ole, moderates engage networks to become advocates for marine stewardship.

Instructive projects, outreach drives, and organizations with nearby partners add to building a feeling of obligation for the prosperity of Ole and its submerged mates. Local area inclusion improves the adequacy of protection gauges and advances feasible practices that benefit the whole coral reef biological system.

Research Drives: Improving Comprehension for Preservation

Research drives zeroed in on Ole's territory inclinations, natural jobs, and reactions to ecological impacts contribute significant information for protection methodologies. Persistent checking of Ole's way of behaving, conceptive elements, and stress reactions gives fundamental information to understanding the species and illuminating proof based preservation measures.

Logical examination likewise assumes a significant part in tending to the more extensive difficulties confronting coral reefs, for example, environmental change, natural surroundings corruption, and the spread of coral sicknesses. The reconciliation of examination discoveries into preservation rehearses upgrades the versatile limit of protection techniques, guaranteeing their significance and adequacy after some time.

Worldwide Coordinated effort: A Bound together Way to deal with Preservation

Given Ole's geographic circulation across various locales and the interconnectedness of marine environments, a worldwide exertion is fundamental for the preservation of its territory and nature. Worldwide cooperation encourages shared research tries, preservation drives, and strategy estimates that add to an aggregate obligation to shielding Ole and safeguarding the biodiversity of coral reefs.

Worldwide drives tending to environmental change, economical turn of events, and the assurance of marine conditions are fundamental for the drawn out protection of Ole and its kindred occupants of coral reefs. A brought together methodology, directed by the standards of environment wellbeing and strength, guarantees that Ole's living space and nature keep on flourishing for people in the future.

3.1 Preferred Reef Environments

The favored reef conditions of Ole, a less popular types of clownfish, unwind a story of particularity and transformation inside the many-sided maze of coral territories. Ole's decision of reef conditions mirrors a finely tuned relationship with the coral designs of the Indo-Pacific, offering bits of knowledge into the environmental subtleties that shape its way of behaving, propagation, and generally endurance.

1. **Coral Design and Microhabitats: Ole's Picked Material**

   Ole, in the same way as other clownfish species, displays areas of strength for a for explicit coral models inside the broad material of the Indo-Pacific reefs. While clownfish, by and large, are known for occupying anemone-related microhabitats, Ole's inclinations dive into the subtleties of coral designs that give cover as well as fundamental assets for its day to day exercises.

   Fanning corals, described by many-sided structures looking like submerged trees, are leaned toward by Ole as essential territories. These fanning developments offer a large number of haven choices, including hole and breaks where Ole can lay out domains, build homes, and look for shelter from likely hunters. The flexibility of Ole to explore through the confounded branches grandstands its advanced ability in taking advantage of the microhabitats given by these coral arrangements.

   As well as fanning corals, Ole may likewise be tracked down in regions with plain corals, described by level, table-like designs. These conditions add to the variety of Ole's favored reef territories, exhibiting its capacity to adjust to changing coral models. The accessibility of plain designs adds a layer of intricacy to Ole's route inside its picked reef conditions, giving various specialties to shield and settling.

2. **Settling Locales: Making Homes Inside the Coral Labyrinth**

   The determination of settling destinations is a urgent part of Ole's favored reef conditions, straightforwardly impacting its regenerative achievement and the propagation of clownfish populaces. Ole, as other clownfish species, is known for its settling ways of behaving, where prevailing females participate in the development and protection of homes for egg statement.

   Inside the favored reef conditions, Ole picks settling locales with explicit qualities that line up with its conceptive requirements. These locales are much of the time situated in shielded regions among the parts of stretching corals, offering security from flows and likely hunters. The nearness to anemones, if accessible, may likewise assume a part in Ole's determination of settling locales, as the cooperative relationship with ocean anemones is necessary to its biology.

   Settling ways of behaving include fastidious readiness of the picked site, with Ole clearing trash and making a level surface reasonable for egg testimony. The presence of appropriate settling destinations inside Ole's favored reef conditions adds to the fruitful generation of clownfish populaces, guaranteeing the continuation of their hereditary inheritance inside the coral reef environment.

3. **Microhabitat Elements: Adjusting to Changing Circumstances**

   Ole's favored reef conditions are not static; they go through powerful changes impacted by variables like water flows, temperature varieties, and associations with other reef occupants. Ole's capacity to adjust to these microhabitat elements is a demonstration of its flexibility inside the consistently moving scene of coral reefs.

   Water flows assume a pivotal part in forming the microhabitat elements of Ole's favored reef conditions. Stretching corals, with their complex designs, make microenvironments where water stream is changed. Ole decisively positions itself inside these microhabitats to exploit decreased current paces, working with productive rummaging and limiting energy use.

   Temperature varieties inside the coral reef climate can impact the microhabitat inclinations of Ole. Coral blanching occasions, connected to raised ocean temperatures, may affect the soundness of fanning corals, adjusting the accessibility of reasonable environments for Ole. Understanding the versatile reactions of Ole to these progressions gives important bits of knowledge into the species' ability to explore and endure inside the powerful states of its favored reef conditions.

   Collaborations with other reef occupants, including contending fish species and possible hunters, additionally add to the microhabitat elements experienced by Ole. The foundation of domains and the essential situating inside coral designs permit Ole to explore these collaborations successfully, guaranteeing admittance to fundamental assets while limiting the dangers related with possible dangers.

4. **Advantageous Affiliations: Anemone-Related Microhabitats**

   While Ole isn't commonly connected with the beneficial interaction with ocean anemones as intently as some other clownfish species, the presence of anemones inside its favored reef conditions adds an interesting aspect to its environment. Anemone-related microhabitats are dynamic spaces where Ole might look for asylum, take part in exceptional ways of behaving, and possibly get extra advantages from the vicinity to these stinging cnidarians.

   Anemones inside Ole's favored reef conditions act as possible safe houses during times of increased weakness, for example, during regional debates or experiences with bigger reef occupants. While Ole doesn't shape elite cooperative associations with anemones to the degree of some other clownfish species, the accessibility of anemones inside its picked living spaces offers an extra layer of intricacy to its biological connections.

   The elements of Ole's collaborations with anemones might include the investigation of the anemone's arms, taking part in ways of behaving that adjust it to the presence of these stinging designs. Ole's flexibility to anemone-related microhabitats features the species' ability to take advantage of accessible assets inside its favored reef conditions, regardless of whether the relationship with anemones isn't quite as cozy as seen in certain other clownfish species.

5. **Profundity Inclinations: Investigating the Upward Aspects**

Ole's favored reef conditions stretch out past the even elements of coral designs; they likewise envelop explicit profundity inclinations that add to the species' dissemination inside the water section. Understanding Ole's upward natural surroundings inclinations reveals insight into its environmental specialty and the variables affecting its spatial dispersion inside the coral reef biological system.

While Ole might be found at different profundities inside the reef, it frequently shows inclinations for explicit profundity goes that line up with its natural requirements. Shallow reef regions, described by spreading corals and plentiful daylight, are leaned toward by Ole for fundamental exercises like rummaging and settling. The accessibility of reasonable settling locales inside these shallow profundities adds to the effective generation of Ole populaces.

At more noteworthy profundities inside the reef, Ole might experience different coral designs and ecological circumstances. The versatility of Ole to investigate these upward aspects mirrors its ability to take advantage of the assets accessible across fluctuating profundity ranges. Factors like light infiltration, water clearness, and the presence of explicit coral species might impact Ole's profundity inclinations inside its picked reef conditions.

6. **Preservation Contemplations: Defending Favored Reef Conditions**

The favored reef conditions of Ole hold significant ramifications for preservation endeavors pointed toward defending the species and the more extensive wellbeing of coral reef biological systems. Perceiving the particular qualities and elements of Ole's picked territories is fundamental for forming viable preservation systems that address the natural complexities of this less popular clownfish species.

Environment Security: Saving the Coral Material

Safeguarding Ole's favored reef conditions requires zeroed in endeavors on environment security. Marine safeguarded regions, where fishing and other human exercises are managed, add to the protection of fundamental settling destinations, microhabitats, and coral designs urgent for Ole's endurance and multiplication.

Feasible fishing rehearses and the relief of anthropogenic stressors, like contamination and territory corruption, are necessary parts of natural surroundings security measures. By guaranteeing the trustworthiness of Ole's picked coral material, moderates add to the general wellbeing and flexibility of coral reef biological systems.

Environmental Change Moderation: Tending to Ecological Elements

The effects of environmental change, including increasing ocean temperatures and coral blanching occasions, straightforwardly impact the elements of Ole's favored reef conditions. Relieving the impacts of environmental change through worldwide drives pointed toward decreasing fossil fuel byproducts and advancing reasonable practices is fundamental for the drawn out protection of Ole and other coral reef occupants.

Tending to environmental change includes lessening ozone harming substance emanations as well as executing systems to upgrade the flexibility of coral reefs to natural stressors. Protection estimates that attention on coral reef rebuilding, checking temperature variances, and elevating versatile administration add to the conservation of Ole's living space despite environment related difficulties.

Examination and Checking: Improving Biological Comprehension

Proceeded with examination and observing endeavors assume an essential part in upgrading how we might interpret Ole's favored reef conditions.

Logical examinations concerning the species' way of behaving, settling elements, and reactions to ecological changes give fundamental information to figuring out proof based protection techniques.

The combination of mechanical devices, like submerged sensors and remote detecting, adds to far reaching checking of coral reef environments. This checking helps with evaluating the wellbeing of Ole's favored reef conditions and recognizing early indications of stress or debasement. Research drives zeroed in on the species additionally add to refining preservation draws near and adjusting systems to the developing natural elements of Ole's living spaces.

Local area Commitment: Promoters for Reef Stewardship

Drawing in neighborhood networks and cultivating schooling are urgent parts of protection endeavors pointed toward safeguarding Ole's favored reef conditions. By bringing issues to light about the novel characteristics and natural significance of Ole, traditionalists engage networks to become advocates for reef stewardship.

Instructive projects, outreach drives, and organizations with neighborhood partners add to building a feeling of obligation for the prosperity of Ole and its kindred occupants of coral reefs. Local area contribution improves the viability of protection gauges and advances manageable practices that benefit Ole as well as the whole coral reef environment.

3.2 Unique Nesting and Breeding Habits

Ole, the less popular types of clownfish, uncovers a captivating section in its life history through its extraordinary settling and reproducing propensities. As an individual from the clownfish family, Ole takes part in ways of behaving that add to the propagation of its species and reflect exceptional variations inside the many-sided scene of coral reef environments.

1. **Home Development: Careful Groundwork for People in the future**

   Home development is a sign of Ole's rearing propensities, and it includes careful planning and joint effort inside the clownfish local area. Predominant females, regularly the biggest people inside the gathering, accept the focal job in building homes. These homes act as defensive sanctuaries for the group of people yet to come of clownfish.

The picked settling destinations are many times arranged inside the protected areas of expanding corals, making a microhabitat that safeguards the creating eggs from expected hunters and natural stressors. Ole's capacity to choose reasonable settling locales inside its favored reef conditions features a degree of flexibility and biological mindfulness fundamental for fruitful proliferation.

The development cycle includes getting the chosen site free from trash and making a level surface where the female can lay her eggs. Ole utilizes its mouth to move and orchestrate little coral sections, displaying accuracy and goal in creating a reasonable climate for its posterity. This careful home arrangement adds to the endurance of the creating eggs and mirrors the significance of parental interest in Ole's rearing procedure.

2. **Conceptive Jobs and Progressive system: A Social Ensemble**

   Ole's rearing propensities are complicatedly woven into the social texture of the clownfish local area, where a progressive design in light of size and regenerative jobs directs the elements of proliferation. The pecking order inside the gathering impacts the distribution of regenerative obligations, with bigger, predominant females expecting the essential rearing jobs.

   The regenerative ordered progression stretches out to the male individuals from the local area, with more modest guys supporting the predominant female in home development and safeguard. This cooperative exertion guarantees the progress of the reproducing pair and adds to the hereditary variety of the clownfish populace inside the coral reef environment.

   The conceptive order isn't static, and changes might happen in view of movements in size and social elements inside the clownfish local area. Understanding the nuanced jobs and collaborations among people inside the gathering gives significant experiences into Ole's rearing propensities and the elements affecting effective multiplication.

3. **Parental Consideration and Safeguard: Watchman of the Clownfish Nursery**

   Ole's reproducing propensities incorporate a wonderful presentation of parental consideration and protection, where both male and female individuals effectively partake in defending the creating eggs. The home, painstakingly developed inside the shielded bounds of spreading corals, turns into a watched nursery kept an eye on by the rearing pair.

   During the hatching time frame, the male and female alternate fanning the eggs with their pectoral blades, guaranteeing a consistent progression of oxygen to the creating undeveloped organisms. This parental consideration is fundamental for the prosperity of the eggs and adds to their effective incubating.

   The defensive way of behaving stretches out past consideration to dynamic safeguard against expected dangers. Ole, especially the male, savagely monitors the home from gatecrashers, including other fish species that might represent a danger to the eggs. The mind boggling dance of parental consideration and guard mirrors the venture of energy and assets Ole devotes to guaranteeing the endurance of its posterity.

4. Coordinated Incubating: A Movement of Life

Ole's rearing propensities incorporate a surprising peculiarity known as coordinated bring forth, where the eggs hatch all the while, leading to a partner of clownfish hatchlings. This synchronized rise isn't just an enamoring show of nature's accuracy yet in addition fills in as a versatile technique for the endurance of the clownfish posterity.

Coordinated bring forth diminishes the weakness of individual hatchlings to predation, as the rise of countless adolescents overpowers expected hunters, improving the probability that some will escape and arrive at more secure zones inside the reef. This organized system improves the endurance possibilities of Ole's posterity during their underlying phases of life in the powerful coral reef climate.

3.3 Interaction with Other Marine Species

Ole, the less popular types of clownfish, takes part in a horde of collaborations with other marine species inside the energetic embroidery of coral reef biological systems. These communications, formed by biological elements and social transformations, add to Ole's endurance, proliferation, and by and large reconciliation into the intricate snare of submerged life.

One of the most interesting connections includes Ole's relationship with ocean anemones. While Ole may not shape selective harmonious organizations with anemones as intently as some other clownfish species, its capacity to look for shelter inside the stinging limbs is critical. Ole's defensive layer of bodily fluid forestalls the nematocysts of the anemone from inflicting damage, permitting it to coincide inside the limbs without setting off a protective reaction. This communication gives Ole a solid haven, and consequently, it might contribute food and supplements to the anemone, displaying a fragile equilibrium of shared benefit.

Ole's searching exercises likewise carry it into contact with a different cluster of marine spineless creatures, zooplankton, and green growth. As an omnivorous feeder, Ole assumes a part in managing the populaces of these life forms inside the coral reef environment. The communications stretch out past simple predation, impacting the elements of prey populaces and adding to the general wellbeing and equilibrium of the submerged local area.

Besides, Ole explores its social scene through connections with other fish species, both inside and outside its clownfish local area. Regional presentations, romance customs, and progressive elements impact these cooperations, molding the social design of Ole's coral reef natural surroundings. These social trades add to the versatility and flexibility of Ole's people group, improving its ability to answer natural changes.

In outline, Ole's communications with other marine species uncover an embroidery of reliance and variation inside the clamoring universe of coral reefs. From looking for shelter inside the appendages of ocean anemones to taking part in the fragile dance of rummaging and social elements, Ole's associations add to the complex orchestra of life that characterizes the submerged domain. Understanding these connections isn't just crucial for logical knowledge yet in addition for the comprehensive preservation and the board of coral reef biological systems where Ole and its marine sidekicks flourish.

Chapter 4

Ole's Role In Coral Ecosystems

Ole, the less popular types of clownfish, expects an essential job in the perplexing dance of life inside coral environments. As an occupant of the Indo-Pacific reefs, Ole's presence resonates through the coral developments, adding to the wellbeing, elements, and flexibility of these energetic submerged networks. In this investigation, we dig into the diverse jobs that Ole plays inside coral environments, from its communications with reef occupants to its effect on the generally biological equilibrium.

1. **Scrounging Elements: Difficult exercise in the Coral Storeroom**
   Ole's job as an omnivorous feeder has broad ramifications for the scrounging elements inside coral biological systems. With a different eating routine that incorporates little spineless creatures, zooplankton, and green growth, Ole effectively partakes in the guideline of prey populaces. This searching way of behaving supports Ole as well as impacts the overflow and conveyance of different creatures inside its natural surroundings.
   The terminal mouth of Ole is finely adjusted for accuracy in catching prey inside the complex designs of coral reefs. Its rummaging exercises add to the fragile equilibrium of coral storage room assets, forestalling overpopulation of specific invertebrate species and advancing biodiversity inside the biological system. Ole's nuanced job in scrounging elements features its situation as a central member in keeping up with the natural balance of coral reefs.

2. **Regional Guardianship: Molding Social Construction and Soundness**
   Territoriality is a characterizing part of Ole's way of behaving, and it assumes a crucial part in forming the social construction and steadiness of coral biological systems. Inside its local area, Ole lays out and shields regions, making spatial spaces for fundamental exercises like taking care of, settling, and romance ceremonies. These domains add to the progressive association of the clownfish local area, with the biggest people frequently accepting predominant jobs.
   Regional guardianship includes visual presentations, including balance develop-

ments, body stances, and even vocalizations, filling in as specialized apparatuses that convey Ole's presence and status inside the social ordered progression. The foundation of regions not just improves the soundness of the clownfish local area yet additionally adds to the versatility and flexibility of coral environments. Ole's job as a regional watchman impacts the spatial elements of the reef, encouraging a harmony among individual and aggregate interests.

3. **Regenerative Elements: Supporting the Ages to Come**

   One of the main commitments of Ole to coral biological systems is its part in conceptive elements. As an animal groups with complex romance customs and settling ways of behaving, Ole effectively takes part in the propagation of clownfish populaces inside its territory. The rearing propensities for Ole are essential to the hereditary variety and flexibility of coral reefs.

   Predominant females, frequently the biggest people inside the gathering, take part in the development and safeguard of homes. Settling locales are painstakingly chosen inside the protected bounds of fanning corals, giving a safe climate to the creating eggs. The synchronized incubating of clownfish hatchlings, worked with by Ole's rearing techniques, adds a layer of intricacy to the regenerative elements of coral environments.

   Ole's part in conceptive elements reaches out past individual rearing matches to impact the hereditary variety of the whole clownfish populace. The various leveled structure inside Ole's people group, in light of size and regenerative jobs, adds to the hereditary strength of the species. Fruitful proliferation guarantees the continuation of Ole's hereditary inheritance and builds up the versatile limit of clownfish populaces inside coral biological systems.

4. **Advantageous Connections: Congruity inside the Coral Ensemble**

   Ole's connections with other marine species, especially its harmonious relationship with ocean anemones, add to the concordance inside the coral orchestra. While Ole may not shape as select a beneficial interaction with anemones as some other clownfish species, its capacity to look for shelter inside the limbs shows a nuanced reliance that improves the environmental texture of coral biological systems.

   The advantageous affiliation includes Ole's defensive variation to the stinging appendages of the anemone. Ole effectively looks for shelter inside the anemone, using a defensive layer of bodily fluid on its skin to keep hurt from the nematocysts. Consequently, Ole gives the anemone food and supplements got from its searching exercises.

   This mutualistic organization adds to the general wellbeing and dependability of coral environments. Ole's presence inside the anemone fills in as an obstruction to likely hunters, upgrading the anemone's security. All the while, Ole benefits from the safe house given by the anemone and gains an essential vantage point for scrounging exercises. This sensitive dance of common advantage inside cooperative connections upgrades the biodiversity and environmental versatility of coral reefs.

5. **Environment Designing: Forming the Submerged Scene**

    Ole's job stretches out to natural surroundings designing, where its ways of behaving impact the actual construction and creation of coral environments. Through home development, regional ways of behaving, and connections with coral arrangements, Ole turns into an unpretentious however effective designer in forming the submerged scene.

    Home development includes the game plan of coral pieces to establish a reasonable climate for egg testimony. This cycle adds to the making of microhabitats inside stretching corals, impacting the geography of the reef and giving protected spaces to the clownfish local area. Ole's job in home development has suggestions for the accessibility of settling destinations and the by and large settling progress of clownfish populaces.

    Regional ways of behaving, including the getting free from trash and the formation of characterized spatial limits, likewise add to natural surroundings designing. Ole's exercises impact the dispersion of assets inside its domain, forming the microenvironments where it scavenges, settles, and cooperates with other reef occupants. These changes to the actual design of the reef mirror Ole's job as an unobtrusive yet significant specialist in the submerged domain.

6. **Biotic Collaborations: Far reaching influences in Coral People group**

    Ole's biotic communications inside coral environments make far reaching influences that resound all through the more extensive local area of reef occupants. As an individual from the clownfish local area, Ole communicates with a different cluster of fish species, spineless creatures, and microorganisms. These communications impact the biological elements of the coral environment, adding to the interconnected snare of life.

    Inside the clownfish local area, Ole's communications with conspecifics (individuals from similar species) and heterospecifics (individuals from various species) shape the social design and ordered progression. Regional debates, romance customs, and helpful ways of behaving impact the spatial circulation and elements of the clownfish populace. Ole's job in these connections adds to the general flexibility and versatility of the clownfish local area inside coral environments.

    Past the clownfish local area, Ole takes part in scavenging collaborations with a different cluster of marine life forms. The guideline of prey populaces through Ole's scrounging exercises impacts the overflow and dispersion of little spineless creatures and zooplankton inside the coral environment. This administrative job has flowing impacts on the more extensive food web, affecting the elements of hunter prey connections and adding to the general equilibrium of the reef local area.

7. **Aversion to Natural Changes: A Bioindicator for Reef Wellbeing**
   Ole's aversion to natural changes positions it as a bioindicator for the well-being and versatility of coral environments. As an animal varieties unpredictably connected to the state of its living space, Ole displays noticeable reactions to varieties in water quality, temperature, and other ecological elements. Checking Ole's ways of behaving and physiological reactions gives significant experiences into the prosperity of the coral reef environment.

   Changes in water quality, like contamination or variances in supplement levels, can get pressure reactions in Ole. These pressure actuated ways of behaving may appear as modifications in tinge, changes in scrounging examples, or changes in regional elements. By noticing and concentrating on these reactions, special-ists and preservationists gain a more profound comprehension of the natural stressors influencing coral biological systems.

   Temperature varieties, incorporating those related with environmental change, likewise impact Ole's way of behaving and prosperity. Increasing ocean tempera-tures can prompt coral dying, influencing the soundness of coral settlements that give fundamental territories to Ole. Observing Ole's reactions to tempera-ture changes fills in as a sign of the more extensive effects of environment related stressors on coral biological systems.

   Ole's aversion to ecological changes highlights the interconnectedness between its prosperity and the general soundness of coral reefs. As a bioindicator, Ole adds to the early location of stressors and gives important data to preservation methodologies pointed toward saving the versatility and versatile limit of coral environments.

8. **Preservation Suggestions: Protecting Ole and Coral Environments**

Understanding Ole's complex job in coral biological systems holds significant ramifications for preservation endeavors pointed toward safeguarding the biodiversity, wellbeing, and flexibility of these submerged domains. As traditionalists explore the intricacies of marine environments, perceiving Ole's commitments becomes instru-mental in figuring out viable techniques that address the particular requirements and elements of this less popular clownfish species.

Territory Insurance: Defending Settling Destinations and Microhabitats
Saving Ole's environment includes centered endeavors around natural surroundings security, especially the settling locales and microhabitats essential for its endurance and multiplication. Marine safeguarded regions, where human exercises are controlled, add to the protection of fundamental rearing and searching reason for Ole.

Environment assurance measures guarantee the accessibility of reasonable settling locales inside expanding corals and add to the protection of microenvironments formed by Ole's regional ways of behaving.

Maintainable fishing rehearses and the relief of anthropogenic stressors, like contamination and territory corruption, are indispensable parts of natural surroundings assurance measures. By guaranteeing the honesty of Ole's picked coral material, progressives add to the general wellbeing and flexibility of coral reef biological systems.

Environmental Change Moderation: Tending to Ecological Stressors

Given Ole's aversion to environment related stressors, including increasing ocean temperatures and coral fading occasions, environmental change alleviation is fundamental for the drawn out preservation of Ole and coral biological systems. Worldwide drives pointed toward lessening fossil fuel byproducts, advancing economical practices, and upgrading the flexibility of coral reefs add to the safeguarding of Ole's living space.

Tending to environmental change includes relieving its effects as well as carrying out methodologies to improve the versatile limit of coral biological systems. Protection estimates that emphasis on coral reef reclamation, observing temperature vacillations, and elevating versatile administration add to the safeguarding of Ole's living space notwithstanding environment related difficulties.

Research Drives: Illuminating Proof Based Preservation

Constant examination drives zeroed in on Ole's way of behaving, settling elements, and reactions to natural changes give fundamental information to prove based preservation techniques. Logical examinations concerning the species add to a more profound comprehension of Ole's part in coral environments and illuminate designated preservation draws near.

Innovative instruments, like submerged sensors, acoustic observing, and satellite symbolism, improve the capacities of analysts to concentrate on Ole and its cooperations inside coral biological systems. Coordinating examination discoveries into preservation rehearses upgrades the versatile limit of protection systems, guaranteeing their pertinence and adequacy over the long run.

Local area Commitment and Training: Supporters for Reef Stewardship

Drawing in nearby networks and cultivating training are fundamental procedures in the protection of Ole and coral biological systems. By bringing issues to light about the one of a kind qualities and environmental significance of Ole, traditionalists engage networks to become advocates for reef stewardship.

Instructive projects, outreach drives, and organizations with neighborhood partners add to building a feeling of obligation for the prosperity of Ole and its kindred occupants of coral reefs. Local area inclusion improves the viability of preservation gauges and advances manageable practices that benefit Ole as well as the whole coral reef environment.

Worldwide Coordinated effort: A Bound together Way to deal with Protection

Given Ole's geographic circulation across various locales and the interconnectedness of marine biological systems, a worldwide exertion is fundamental for the protection of its territory and commitments to coral environments. Global cooperation cultivates shared research tries, protection drives, and strategy estimates that add to an aggregate obligation to defending Ole and saving the biodiversity of coral reefs.

Worldwide drives tending to environmental change, maintainable turn of events, and the assurance of marine conditions are fundamental for the drawn out protection of Ole and its kindred occupants of coral reefs. A bound together methodology, directed by the standards of environment wellbeing and strength, guarantees that Ole's job in coral biological systems keeps on flourishing for people in the future.

4.1Symbiotic Relationships with Anemones

Inside the unpredictable expressive dance of the coral reef biological system, Ole, the less popular types of clownfish, takes part in an enrapturing cooperative relationship with ocean anemones. This organization, portrayed by common advantage and perplexing variations, uncovers a dance of congruity that enhances the submerged embroidery. In this investigation, we dig into the nuanced elements of Ole's advantageous associations with anemones, revealing insight into the complexities that characterize this spellbinding coalition.

1. **The Dance of Security: Ole's Shelter inside the Anemone's Hug**

   The cooperative connection among Ole and ocean anemones is established in the dance of security, where each accomplice gives one of a kind benefits to the next. Ocean anemones, equipped with stinging limbs, offer Ole a defensive shelter against expected hunters. The limbs, loaded down with particular cells called nematocysts, can convey a powerful sting to interlopers.

   Notwithstanding, Ole has a wonderful variation that permits it to explore the anemone's limbs safe. A defensive layer of bodily fluid on Ole's skin forestalls the nematocysts from terminating upon contact, conceding it resistance to the stinging safeguards of the ocean anemone. This unpredictable transformation empowers Ole to look for shelter inside the anemone's hug, using its limbs as a safeguard against bigger reef occupants that could represent a danger.

   The dance of security unfurls as Ole, with its lively tones and particular examples, consolidates flawlessly with the appendages of the ocean anemone. As a trade-off for this safe-haven, Ole adds to the anemone's prosperity through a unique trade of assets and ways of behaving.

2. **The Artful dance of Supplement Trade: Anemone's Abundance from Ole's Searching Accomplishments**

   The cooperative organization reaches out past simple security, developing into an expressive dance of supplement trade where Ole effectively adds to the sustenance of the ocean anemone. Ole's omnivorous eating routine, which incorporates little spineless creatures, zooplankton, and green growth, turns into a wellspring of food for the anemone inside its tentacular hug.

   As Ole rummages inside the coral reef environment, it catches and consumes little prey things, acclimatizing supplements fundamental for its own endurance. However, the unique interaction of the harmonious relationship comes to the very front as Ole moves a part of these gained supplements to the ocean anemone. Through waste and other metabolic results, Ole enhances the water encompassing the anemone, furnishing it with fundamental components for development and food.

In this expressive dance of supplement trade, Ole turns into an essential supporter of the prosperity of the ocean anemone. The organization rises above a simple safe house game plan to a commonly valuable dynamic, where Ole's searching accomplishments straightforwardly impact the wholesome scene of the anemone's microenvironment.

3. **The Beautiful Dance of Cover: Anemone and Ole together as one**

   The visual exhibition of Ole's dynamic tones and mind boggling designs entwining with the ocean anemone shapes an expressive dance of disguise that serves the two accomplices in the cooperative relationship. Ole's appearance, decorated with striking tints and unmistakable markings, adds to the anemone's general disguise methodology inside the coral reef environment.

   Ocean anemones, in spite of their stinging arms, are not resistant to predation. Certain reef occupants, like butterflyfish and angelfish, display a distinct fascination with consuming ocean anemones. Ole's presence inside the anemone's limbs adds a layer of cover that benefits the two accomplices. The energetic shades of Ole mix with the anemone's own pigmentation, making an outwardly agreeable presentation that hides the clownfish from possible hunters.

   This artful dance of cover is a powerful transformation that improves the endurance possibilities of both Ole and the ocean anemone. While Ole acquires security from hunters through the anemone's limbs, the anemone, thus, benefits from Ole's presence as a living cover that lessens its weakness to predation.

4. **The Movement of Anemone Investigation: Ole's Connection with Limbs**

   Ole's harmonious relationship with ocean anemones includes a fragile movement of investigation, where the clownfish draws in with the limbs in a progression of ways of behaving that adjust it to the stinging designs. Not at all like some other clownfish species that structure more select advantageous bonds with anemones, Ole's association with these cnidarian accomplices is more transient and sharp.

   Ole displays ways of behaving that include cautious and purposeful contact with the anemone's limbs. Through material investigation, Ole gets comfortable with the design and responsiveness of the arms, adjusting itself to the potential dangers presented by the nematocysts. This movement of anemone investigation is a nuanced show of Ole's flexibility to its harmonious accomplice.

   While Ole may not foster similar level of protection from the stinging cells as other clownfish species, its communications with the anemone's limbs add to a shared grasping between the accomplices. Ole's exploratory ways of behaving exhibit the species' capacity to explore the possibly dangerous landscape of the anemone's hug, featuring the flexibility inborn in this powerful harmonious relationship.

5. **The Harmonious Two part harmony: Conceptive Ramifications in Clownfish-Anemone Associations**

   The cooperative connection among Ole and ocean anemones takes on an especially fascinating aspect while considering the regenerative ramifications for clownfish species. While Ole may not shape as restrictive a beneficial interaction with anemones as some other clownfish species, the presence of anemones inside its territory adds a layer of intricacy to its regenerative techniques.

   In certain clownfish species, the determination of settling locales is impacted by the nearness of ocean anemones. The defensive appendages of the anemone offer an additional layer of safety for the clownfish during the weak phases of egg affidavit and hatching. The presence of anemones might impact Ole's decisions in settling destinations, adding to the regenerative achievement and endurance of its posterity.

   The advantageous two part harmony among Ole and ocean anemones in the domain of proliferation isn't quite as articulated as in some other clownfish-anemone organizations. By the by, the possible impact of anemones on settling ways of behaving and site choice highlights the nuanced and interconnected nature of harmonious connections inside the coral reef environment.

6. **Variations and Specificities: Ole's Extraordinary Way to deal with Advantageous interaction**

   Ole's way to deal with cooperative associations with ocean anemones features a novel arrangement of transformations and specificities that recognize it from other clownfish species.

   While Ole participates in a harmonious hit the dance floor with anemones, the profundity and selectiveness of this relationship might shift, featuring the versatility of clownfish species to their particular environmental specialties.

   One vital transformation is Ole's capacity to explore the appendages of ocean anemones without shaping select and profoundly safe bonds to the stinging designs. This flexibility permits Ole to look for shelter inside the anemone's hug when required, profiting from the security presented by the limbs, without shaping a super durable home.

   Ole's harmonious methodology is entrepreneurial, impacted by elements, for example, settling necessities, searching techniques, and the generally biological setting of its territory. The species exhibits an adaptability that permits it to take part in harmonious collaborations with anemones as a component of its collection of step by step processes for surviving inside the coral reef environment.

7. **Preservation Contemplations: Saving Harmonious Organizations in Coral Reefs**

Understanding the complexities of Ole's harmonious associations with ocean anemones holds huge ramifications for the preservation of coral reef biological systems. As these submerged domains face different dangers, including territory debasement, environmental change, and overfishing, saving harmonious organizations becomes urgent for the wellbeing and versatility of coral networks.

Natural surroundings Security: Defending Anemone Habitations

Safeguarding Ole's cooperative associations with ocean anemones includes designated endeavors to safeguard the territories where anemones flourish. Marine safeguarded regions, where human exercises are directed, add to the preservation of fundamental anemone homes. Territory insurance measures guarantee the accessibility of reasonable conditions for both Ole and ocean anemones, cultivating the continuation of their advantageous dance.

Manageable Fishing Works on: Moderating Anthropogenic Stressors

Embracing manageable fishing rehearses is fundamental for relieving anthropogenic stressors that can disturb Ole's cooperative connections. Overfishing, disastrous fishing strategies, and the evacuation of key reef occupants can adversely influence the fragile equilibrium of cooperative associations inside coral biological systems.

Protection drives that advance maintainable fishing rehearses add to the general soundness of coral reefs, permitting Ole and its advantageous accomplices to flourish. By tending to the human-instigated stressors on marine conditions, these drives make a more favorable setting for the mind boggling expressive dance of harmonious connections to unfurl.

Environmental Change Moderation: Safeguarding Biological system Versatility

Given the powerlessness of coral reefs to environmental change, moderation methodologies are fundamental for protecting the flexibility of Ole's cooperative associations. Worldwide drives pointed toward diminishing fossil fuel byproducts, safeguarding coral territories, and upgrading the versatile limit of marine environments add to the drawn out protection of these complex connections.

Tending to the effects of environmental change includes relieving its belongings as well as executing procedures to improve the flexibility of coral biological systems. Protection estimates that emphasis on coral reef rebuilding, observing temperature variances, and elevating versatile administration add to the safeguarding of Ole's advantageous dance inside changing natural circumstances.

Examination and Observing: Disentangling Harmonious Secrets

Proceeded with exploration and checking endeavors assume a crucial part in unwinding the secrets of Ole's cooperative associations with ocean anemones. Logical examinations concerning the species' way of behaving, conceptive elements, and reactions to natural changes give fundamental information to confirm based protection procedures.

The reconciliation of innovative apparatuses, like submerged sensors, acoustic checking, and hereditary examinations, improves the capacities of analysts to concentrate on Ole and its collaborations inside advantageous organizations. Research drives zeroed in on the species add to a more profound comprehension of its job in coral biological systems and illuminate designated protection draws near.

Public Mindfulness and Training: Supporting for Reef Stewardship

Raising public mindfulness and encouraging schooling are fundamental parts of preservation endeavors pointed toward protecting Ole's advantageous connections. By featuring the novel qualities and biological significance of Ole and its organizations with ocean anemones, preservationists engage networks to become advocates for reef stewardship.

Instructive projects, outreach drives, and organizations with nearby partners add to building a feeling of obligation for the prosperity of Ole and its cooperative accomplices inside coral reefs. Public mindfulness crusades advance reasonable practices that benefit Ole as well as the whole coral reef environment.

4.2 Impact on Coral Health and Growth

Ole, the less popular types of clownfish, plays a nuanced and effective job in the wellbeing and development of coral reefs. This advantageous relationship stretches out past Ole's cooperations with ocean anemones, affecting the general elements of coral biological systems.

Understanding the particular manners by which Ole adds to coral wellbeing and development reveals insight into the many-sided interaction among clownfish and their coral natural surroundings.

1. **Scavenging Elements and Coral Wellbeing: The Equilibrium of Nature**

   Ole's omnivorous eating regimen, which incorporates little spineless creatures, zooplankton, and green growth, adds to the guideline of prey populaces inside the coral reef environment. This scrounging conduct straightforwardly affects coral wellbeing by forestalling the excess of specific organic entities that could somehow contend with corals for space and assets.

   In the fragile equilibrium of nature, Ole's job as a forager keeps a sound harmony inside the coral storeroom. By controlling the wealth of possibly hurtful spineless creatures and green growth, Ole in a roundabout way cultivates a better climate for coral development. This part of Ole's impact highlights the interconnected connections inside coral biological systems, where the prosperity of one animal categories can have flowing consequences for the whole local area.

2. **Regional Guardianship and Coral Solidness: A Reef Safehaven**

   Ole's regional ways of behaving, set apart by the foundation and protection of domains inside the coral reef, add to the dependability and wellbeing of coral networks. By making spatial areas for fundamental exercises like taking care of, settling, and romance ceremonies, Ole improves the spatial association of the reef.

   In the domain of coral wellbeing and development, Ole's regional guardianship fills in as a defensive layer. The distinct domains go about as places of refuge where coral states can prosper without the gamble of unreasonable aggravations.

The dependability achieved by Ole's presence adds to the strength of coral reefs, permitting them to really endure ecological stressors and aggravations more.

3. **Home Development and Microhabitat Arrangement: Coral-Accommodating Conditions**

   Ole's settling ways of behaving include the careful development of homes inside the shielded bounds of stretching corals. This interaction makes microhabitats that not just act as defensive spaces for clownfish posterity yet in addition add to the wellbeing and development of the encompassing coral provinces.

   The game plan of coral parts during home development can impact the actual construction of the reef, making level surfaces and protected spaces that are helpful for coral settlement and development. Ole's settling exercises, in this manner, assume a part in the development of coral-accommodating conditions, giving reasonable substrates to coral hatchlings connection and adding to the general design and flexibility of the reef.

4. **Cooperative Connections and Coral Flexibility: Anemones as Accomplices in Development**

While Ole may not shape as selective a beneficial interaction with ocean anemones as some other clownfish species, the presence of these cnidarian accomplices inside Ole's environment has suggestions for coral strength. Ocean anemones, with their stinging appendages and defensive designs, can make microenvironments that benefit coral wellbeing.

Ole's advantageous communications with ocean anemones add an extra layer to the complicated mosaic of coral reef elements. The likely impact of anemones on settling ways of behaving and site choice by Ole adds to the general strength and flexibility of coral environments. In this specific circumstance, Ole's presence inside the cooperative dance further underlines the interconnected connections that shape the development and wellbeing of coral reefs.

4.3 Ecological Significance of Ole's Behavior

Ole, the less popular types of clownfish, unfurls an embroidery of natural importance through its mind boggling ways of behaving inside the coral reef biological system. From searching elements to regional guardianship, Ole's conduct collection assumes a crucial part in forming the biological equilibrium and strength of coral reefs.

1. **Scavenging Elements: Directing Prey Populaces**

   Ole's omnivorous eating regimen and searching ways of behaving add to the guideline of prey populaces inside the coral reef biological system. As a proficient hunter of little spineless creatures, zooplankton, and green growth, Ole assumes an essential part in controlling the overflow of specific organic entities that could somehow multiply and contend with corals for space and assets. This rummaging dynamic makes a sensitive equilibrium in the coral storage room, impacting the general wellbeing and variety of the reef local area.

2. **Regional Guardianship: Upgrading Spatial Association**
   Ole's regional ways of behaving include the foundation and safeguard of explicit regions inside the coral reef. This regional guardianship improves the spatial association of the reef, making clear cut zones for fundamental exercises like taking care of, settling, and romance customs. The strength achieved by Ole's regional presence adds to the general soundness of coral reefs by limiting unsettling influences and giving places of refuge to coral development.

3. **Home Development: Microhabitat Arrangement**
   The careful development of homes by Ole inside spreading corals adds to the arrangement of microhabitats. These settling locales act as defensive spaces for clownfish posterity and establish organized conditions inside the reef. The plan of coral pieces during home development impacts the actual construction of the coral natural surroundings, giving appropriate substrates to coral hatchlings connection and adding to the general variety and strength of the reef.

4. **Harmonious Connections: Anemones as Biological system Patrons**

While Ole may not shape as selective an advantageous interaction with ocean anemones as some other clownfish species, its connections with these cnidarian accomplices have biological ramifications. Ocean anemones, with their stinging arms and defensive designs, make microenvironments that benefit coral wellbeing. Ole's presence inside the harmonious dance adds an extra layer to the mind boggling mosaic of coral reef elements, adding to the general versatility and flexibility of the biological system.

Basically, Ole's ways of behaving resonate through the coral reef biological system, affecting the unpredictable trap of connections and adding to the environmental woven artwork that characterizes these submerged domains. As preservation endeavors look to comprehend and protect the biological meaning of Ole's way of behaving, they assume a crucial part in defending the wellbeing and strength of coral reefs for people in the future.

Chapter 5

Conservation Status And Threats

As a less popular types of clownfish, Ole occupies the energetic coral reefs of the Indo-Pacific, adding to the complicated environmental equilibrium of these submerged domains. In any case, in the same way as other marine species, Ole faces a horde of dangers that challenge its endurance. Figuring out the preservation status and distinguishing the key dangers is foremost to forming successful methodologies to safeguard this unexpected, yet invaluable treasure of the reef.

Preservation Status of Ole: Disclosing the Unlikely treasure's Weakness

Ole's protection status is a fundamental beginning stage in tending to the difficulties looked by this less popular clownfish species. While explicit appraisals might fluctuate, Ole for the most part falls inside the more extensive class of marine species confronting protection concerns. The Worldwide Association for Preservation of Nature (IUCN) gives a system to assessing the elimination hazard of species, including marine living beings like Ole.

The preservation status of Ole is impacted by elements, for example, populace size, conveyance, living space corruption, and powerlessness to different dangers. Given the mind boggling environmental jobs Ole plays inside coral biological systems, understanding its protection status is pivotal for safeguarding the biodiversity and strength of these submerged domains.

Dangers Confronting Ole: Exploring the Risks of the Submerged Domain

1. **Territory Debasement and Misfortune: Sabotaging the Coral Material**
   Territory debasement is an essential danger to Ole and other coral reef occupants. Human exercises, for example, overfishing, disastrous fishing rehearses, and waterfront improvement add to the decay of coral reefs. Ole's reliance on complicated coral arrangements for settling and sanctuary makes it especially defenseless against the misfortune and corruption of these living spaces.
   Coral blanching, a peculiarity exacerbated by increasing ocean temperatures and environmental change, represents an extreme danger to Ole's living space.

60

Dyed corals are debilitated and more defenseless to infections, diminishing their reasonableness for Ole's settling and regional ways of behaving. Preservation endeavors should address living space security and reclamation to neutralize the effect of natural surroundings corruption on Ole's endurance.

2. **Environmental Change: The Worldwide Danger Amplifying Neighborhood Risks**

   Environmental change intensifies the dangers confronting Ole and coral reefs at a worldwide scale. Increasing ocean temperatures add to coral fading, modifying the elements of the submerged environment. Sea fermentation, one more outcome of environmental change, can influence the accessibility of calcium carbonate for coral development, impeding the improvement of appropriate settling locales for Ole.

   Ocean level ascent, driven by environmental change, represents an immediate danger to the waterfront natural surroundings fundamental for Ole's endurance. As ocean levels increment, the shallow reefs where Ole flourishes might be lowered, influencing the accessibility of reasonable conditions for settling and scavenging. Tending to environmental change is urgent for alleviating these worldwide dangers and shielding Ole's territory.

3. **Overfishing and Impractical Works on: Upsetting the Clownfish People group**

   Overfishing and impractical fishing rehearses add to the exhaustion of marine assets, affecting Ole by implication through interruptions to the clownfish local area. Expulsion of key species from the biological system can make lopsided characteristics, influencing the accessibility of food assets and changing the elements of cooperations inside the reef.

   The aquarium exchange, where clownfish are well known decisions for home aquariums, represents an immediate danger to Ole. Unregulated assortment for the pet exchange can drain nearby populaces and disturb the social construction of clownfish networks. Executing economical fishing works on, directing the aquarium exchange, and laying out marine safeguarded regions are fundamental for relieving the effects of overfishing on Ole.

4. **Contamination: The Undetectable Danger in Submerged Domains**

   Marine contamination, including plastic trash, oil slicks, and overflow from land-based exercises, represents an unavoidable danger to Ole and its coral living space. The amassing of plastic waste can ensnare marine life, including clownfish, while oil slicks can harmfully affect both grown-up and larval phases of Ole.

   Supplement spillover from agrarian and metropolitan regions can prompt coral reef corruption, affecting water quality and advancing the development of destructive green growth. Ole's aversion to ecological changes, especially varieties in water quality, makes it defenseless to the negative impacts of contamination. Preservation endeavors should address contamination counteraction and the executives to safeguard Ole and its coral natural surroundings.

5. The travel industry Effect: Adjusting Preservation and Amusement

The travel industry, while giving financial advantages, can likewise present dangers to Ole and coral reefs. Actual harm from exercises, for example, stomping on, anchor harm, and imprudent treatment of marine life can straightforwardly influence the coral natural surroundings and disturb Ole's ways of behaving. Moreover, the assortment of clownfish for the aquarium exchange, frequently determined by traveler interest, can add to populace decline.

Carrying out feasible the travel industry works on, upholding guidelines to limit actual effect, and bringing issues to light among guests about dependable conduct in marine conditions are fundamental parts of protection procedures. Adjusting the financial advantages of the travel industry with the need to safeguard Ole and its natural surroundings is significant for long haul preservation achievement.

Protection Techniques for Ole: Supporting the Unexpected, yet invaluable treasure

Saving Ole and guaranteeing the wellbeing and flexibility of coral reefs request far reaching protection techniques that address the particular dangers confronting this unexpected, yet invaluable treasure of the reef. The accompanying methodologies frame a guide for compelling preservation:

1. **Natural surroundings Security and Rebuilding: Shielding the Coral Material**

   Starting and growing marine safeguarded regions (MPAs) can give basic shelter to Ole and its coral natural surroundings. MPAs direct human exercises, taking into account regular cycles of recuperation and advancing the versatility of coral environments. Rebuilding endeavors, including coral transplantation and living space recovery, add to the reclamation of reasonable conditions for Ole's settling and rummaging ways of behaving.

2. **Environmental Change Relief: A Worldwide Goal**

   Worldwide endeavors to relieve environmental change are basic for safeguarding Ole and coral reefs. Promotion for decreased fossil fuel byproducts, reasonable energy practices, and environment versatility drives can address the underlying drivers of environmental change. Nearby and global coordinated efforts are crucial for execute methodologies that upgrade the versatile limit of coral biological systems, permitting Ole to flourish in the midst of changing natural circumstances.

3. **Economical Fishing Works on: Adjusting Harvest and Protection**

   Carrying out and authorizing reasonable fishing rehearses are critical for keeping up with the equilibrium of the clownfish local area and saving Ole.

   Guidelines that breaking point get sizes, safeguard key reproducing regions, and screen the effect of fishing exercises add to the practical administration of marine assets. Instructing neighborhood networks and fishers about the significance of reasonable practices cultivates a feeling of stewardship towards Ole and the more extensive marine environment.

4. **Contamination Anticipation and The executives: Safeguarding Water Quality**

Diminishing contamination requires a diverse methodology, including waste decrease, worked on squander the executives, and the implementation of ecological guidelines. Public mindfulness missions can teach networks about the effect of contamination on Ole and coral reefs, cultivating a feeling of obligation for safeguarding marine conditions. Coordinated effort between state run administrations, enterprises, and neighborhood networks is fundamental for successful contamination anticipation and the executives.

5. **The travel industry The board: Adjusting Diversion and Protection**

Supportable the travel industry rehearses are fundamental to limiting the effect of human exercises on Ole and coral reefs. Executing and authorizing rules for mindful marine the travel industry, including the denial of disastrous practices and the advancement of eco-accommodating exercises, add to preservation endeavors. Drawing in neighborhood networks in the travel industry the executives guarantees that financial advantages are offset with the protection of Ole and its natural surroundings.

6. **Exploration and Checking: Illuminating Proof Based Protection**

Persistent exploration drives zeroed in on Ole's way of behaving, conceptive elements, and reactions to natural changes give fundamental information to prove based preservation methodologies. Logical examinations concerning the species add to a more profound comprehension of Ole's job in coral biological systems, illuminating designated preservation draws near. Observing the well-being and populace patterns of Ole and its advantageous accomplices upgrades the versatile limit of preservation techniques, guaranteeing their importance and viability after some time.

7. **Local area Commitment and Instruction: Encouraging Stewardship**

Connecting with nearby networks and encouraging schooling are fundamental procedures in the preservation of Ole and coral biological systems. By bringing issues to light about the special qualities and natural significance of Ole, preservationists engage networks to become advocates for reef stewardship. Instructive projects, outreach drives, and organizations with nearby partners add to building a feeling of obligation for the prosperity of Ole and its kindred occupants of coral reefs.

8. **Global Coordinated effort: A Brought together Way to deal with Preservation**

Given Ole's geographic dissemination across various districts and the interconnectedness of marine environments, a worldwide exertion is fundamental for the preservation of its natural surroundings and commitments to coral biological systems. Worldwide coordinated effort cultivates shared research tries, protection drives, and strategy estimates that add to an aggregate obligation to defending Ole and safeguarding the biodiversity of coral reefs.

5.1 Evaluation of Ole's Population Trends

Understanding the populace patterns of Ole, the less popular types of clownfish, is a vital part of surveying its protection status and the general strength of coral reef biological systems. The assessment of populace patterns includes a complete assessment of elements like dissemination, overflow, conceptive achievement, and reaction to natural changes. In this investigation, we dive into the many-sided elements of Ole's populace patterns, revealing insight into the difficulties, potential open doors, and bits of knowledge that rise up out of concentrating on this unlikely treasure of the reef.

Conveyance Examples: Planning Ole's Submerged Domain

The appropriation of Ole gives significant bits of knowledge into the species' biological inclinations, environment necessities, and likely weaknesses. Leading overviews and submerged appraisals across the Indo-Pacific district permits analysts to plan the regions where Ole populaces are flourishing, recognize key territories, and comprehend the elements impacting their conveyance.

Ole's dissemination might change in view of variables, for example, water temperature, coral reef structure, and the accessibility of appropriate settling locales. Thorough planning endeavors add to a more clear comprehension of the geographic scope of Ole, assisting progressives with focusing on unambiguous regions for insurance and the board.

Overflow and Populace Thickness: Measuring Ole's Presence

Evaluating the overflow and populace thickness of Ole includes quantitative studies and observing methods. Specialists use techniques, for example, submerged visual censuses, hereditary examinations, and acoustic checking to appraise populace sizes and track changes over the long haul. These evaluations give important information on the overall overflow of Ole in various reef conditions and deal experiences into likely changes.

Checking populace thickness is fundamental for measuring the conveying limit of territories and understanding how Ole associates with its current circumstance. Factors like rivalry for assets, regional ways of behaving, and regenerative achievement add to varieties in populace thickness, and concentrating on these elements upgrades how we might interpret Ole's job inside the more extensive coral reef local area.

Regenerative Achievement: Divulging the Mysteries of Ole's Life Cycle

Ole's regenerative achievement is a vital determinant of populace patterns and long haul suitability. The species' life cycle includes perplexing ways of behaving connected with romance, settling, and parental consideration. Checking regenerative achievement incorporates evaluating elements, for example, the recurrence of generating occasions, egg endurance rates, and the enrollment of new people into the populace.

Romance ceremonies, which might incorporate elaborate moves and ways of behaving, add to the development of reproducing matches and the ensuing outcome of settling. Noticing these ways of behaving permits scientists to acquire experiences into the regenerative systems of Ole and what they might be meant for by natural circumstances.

Settling achievement is a basic part of Ole's populace elements. The cautious development and support of homes inside coral branches give security to eggs and hatchlings. Checking the endurance paces of eggs and the effective bring forth of hatchlings add to how we might interpret the difficulties Ole faces during the beginning phases of its life cycle.

Understanding the variables that impact conceptive achievement is essential for anticipating the strength of Ole populaces even with ecological stressors. Changes in ocean temperature, living space debasement, and different dangers can affect the progress of bringing forth occasions and the endurance of posterity, impacting the general populace patterns of Ole.

Reaction to Natural Changes: Versatility Despite Difficulties

Ole's reaction to natural changes is a basic part of assessing its populace patterns. Coral reefs, the essential territory of Ole, are especially helpless to natural stressors, for example, environmental change, contamination, and living space debasement. Evaluating how Ole populaces answer these difficulties gives bits of knowledge into the species' flexibility and strength.

Changes in water temperature, an outcome of environmental change, can impact the circulation and conduct of Ole. Coral blanching occasions, set off by raised ocean temperatures, may influence the accessibility of appropriate settling locales and effect the soundness of coral reef environments.

Concentrating on how Ole populaces answer these temperature variances illuminates preservation systems pointed toward relieving the effects of environmental change on the species.

Contamination, including plastic garbage and supplement spillover, can likewise present dangers to Ole and its territory. Evaluating the presence of toxins and their impacts on Ole populaces distinguishes regions where preservation endeavors ought to zero in on moderating human-actuated stressors. Understanding how Ole explores and adjusts to changes in water quality is fundamental for creating successful protection measures.

Challenges in Populace Observing: Exploring the Profundities of Information Assortment

While assessing Ole's populace patterns is pivotal for protection endeavors, there are innate difficulties in checking an animal categories that occupies the mind boggling and dynamic climate of coral reefs. The submerged domain presents strategic difficulties for analysts, including restricted perceivability, admittance to distant areas, and the requirement for specific hardware.

Evaluating the wealth of Ole, particularly inside perplexing reef structures, requires progressed study methods and innovations. Submerged visual censuses might be restricted by the species' enigmatic nature, and hereditary examinations might give more exact populace gauges. Nonetheless, these techniques frequently require huge assets and mastery.

Concentrating on Ole's conceptive achievement can be trying because of the cryptic idea of settling ways of behaving. Getting to and checking homes inside coral branches requires cautious route and non-meddlesome perception strategies. Mechanical headways, for example, submerged cameras and sensors, assume a urgent part in defeating these difficulties and getting important information on Ole's regenerative elements.

The reaction of Ole populaces to natural changes presents one more layer of intricacy. The interconnected idea of coral reef biological systems implies that adjustments of one part, like ocean temperature or water quality, can have flowing consequences for Ole and its cooperative accomplices. Incorporating information from various sources, including natural checking and species cooperations, upgrades how we might interpret the mind boggling elements at play.

Open doors for Future Exploration: Diagramming the Course for Ole's Preservation

As we explore the profundities of understanding Ole's populace drifts, a few open doors arise for future exploration that can improve preservation techniques and add to the more extensive comprehension of coral reef biological systems:

1. **High level Checking Advances: Developments in Information Assortment**
   Proceeded with progressions in observing advancements offer promising open doors for concentrating on Ole right at home. The improvement of submerged drones, independent submerged vehicles (AUVs), and remotely worked vehicles (ROVs) empowers analysts to investigate and screen reef conditions with more prominent accuracy. These innovations improve the effectiveness and precision of information assortment, giving a more thorough image of Ole's populace elements.

2. **Hereditary Examinations: Disentangling the Variety Inside Ole Populaces**
   Hereditary examinations offer an incredible asset for disentangling the variety inside Ole populaces. Concentrating on the hereditary design of populaces gives bits of knowledge into network between various reef areas, levels of hereditary variety, and the potential for transformation to ecological changes. This data is important for planning protection procedures that focus on hereditarily different populaces and improve the general versatility of Ole.

3. **Long haul Observing: Following Patterns Across Ages**
   Long haul observing drives give the potential chance to follow populace patterns across different ages of Ole. Laying out checking programs that range quite a

while permits specialists to recognize patterns, survey the effect of protection mediations, and comprehend the species' reaction to long haul natural changes. Long haul informational collections add to the improvement of prescient models that can direct protection endeavors into what's in store.

4. **Conduct Studies: Bits of knowledge Into Ole's Variations and Collaborations**

   Top to bottom conduct concentrates on offer chances to acquire experiences into Ole's transformations and communications inside the coral reef environment. Perceptions of romance customs, settling ways of behaving, and regional elements give a more profound comprehension of the species' life history and social construction. Social examinations contribute important data for planning preservation methodologies that think about the particular natural prerequisites and ways of behaving of Ole.

5. **Local area Inclusion: Resident Science and Nearby Information**

Including nearby networks and resident researchers in populace checking endeavors presents an important chance to accumulate information across a more extensive geographic reach. Neighborhood information about Ole's ways of behaving, dispersion, and environmental connections can supplement logical exploration and add to a more comprehensive comprehension of populace patterns. Local area inclusion likewise encourages a feeling of stewardship and can uphold preservation drives at the grassroots level.

5.2 Human Impact on Ole's Habitat

The flawless magnificence of coral reefs, Ole's regular natural surroundings, is progressively compromised by a scope of human-prompted influences. As the complicated environments that help a rich variety of marine life, coral reefs are helpless against a heap of stressors originating from human exercises. Understanding the particular manners by which human effect influences Ole's living space is significant for figuring out compelling preservation systems that safeguard the sensitive equilibrium of these submerged domains.

1. **Environment Debasement: Sabotaging Ole's Protecting Home**

   Human exercises, both beach front and seaward, contribute altogether to the corruption of Ole's natural surroundings. Beach front turn of events, contamination, and impractical fishing rehearses are key drivers of environment misfortune and debasement.

   Beach front turn of events, frequently determined by the travel industry and urbanization, prompts living space annihilation through exercises, for example, digging, land recovery, and the development of marinas. These modifications to the shore straightforwardly influence the accessibility and nature of the shallow reef conditions that Ole depends on for cover, settling, and scrounging.

Contamination, including sedimentation, supplement overflow, and marine flotsam and jetsam, represents an extreme danger to Ole's territory. Sedimentation, coming about because of exercises like development and deforestation, can cover coral reefs, influencing their wellbeing and lessening the accessibility of reasonable surfaces for Ole's settling ways of behaving. Supplement spillover from horticultural and metropolitan regions can prompt algal sprouts, affecting water quality and rivaling corals for space.

Marine trash, especially plastic waste, represents an immediate danger to Ole and its living space. Snare in disposed of fishing gear and the ingestion of plastic particles can hurt Ole and other reef occupants. The diligence of plastic trash in the sea worsens the difficulties looked by Ole's territory, undermining its biological honesty.

2. **Environmental Change: Raised Dangers to Ole's Submerged Home**

Environmental change is a worldwide danger that essentially influences Ole's natural surroundings and the more extensive soundness of coral reef biological systems. Increasing ocean temperatures, sea fermentation, and outrageous climate occasions are ramifications of environmental change that posture raised dangers to Ole's submerged home.

Raised ocean temperatures add to coral fading, a peculiarity where cooperative green growth residing inside coral tissues are ousted, prompting the deficiency of lively varieties and expanded vulnerability to illnesses.

Coral fading occasions debilitate the underlying uprightness of coral reefs, affecting the accessibility of reasonable living spaces for Ole. As Ole depends on solid coral developments for settling and sanctuary, the debasement of coral reefs straightforwardly influences its endurance.

Sea fermentation, coming about because of the ingestion of overabundance carbon dioxide via seawater, can obstruct the development and advancement of coral skeletons. As Ole's territory is unpredictably associated with the actual design of coral reefs, the effect of sea fermentation on coral wellbeing has roundabout ramifications for the accessibility of appropriate conditions for settling and regional ways of behaving.

Outrageous climate occasions, like storms and twisters, can make actual harm coral reefs. The obliteration of coral designs and the interruption of reef biological systems can have flowing impacts on Ole's natural surroundings, affecting its capacity to find appropriate settling destinations and explore inside the reef.

3. **Overfishing and Unreasonable Works on: Upsetting the Clownfish People group**

Overfishing and unreasonable fishing rehearses straightforwardly influence Ole's territory by disturbing the sensitive equilibrium of the clownfish local area and the more extensive coral reef biological system. Expulsion of key species from the environment can prompt irregular characteristics in populace elements, influencing the accessibility of food assets and modifying the associations inside the reef.

Unregulated and disastrous fishing rehearses, for example, impact fishing and cyanide fishing, can make actual harm coral reefs. The utilization of these strategies to get fish for the aquarium exchange represents an immediate danger to Ole. The expulsion of people from the clownfish local area can upset social designs and lead to the decay of nearby populaces.

4. **The travel industry Effect: Exploring a Difficult exercise**

The travel industry, while giving monetary advantages to waterfront networks, can likewise affect Ole's natural surroundings. Actual harm from exercises, for example, stomping on, anchor harm, and flippant swimming or plunging practices can hurt coral reefs. The prevalence of clownfish, including Ole, in the aquarium exchange might drive assortment pressures, especially in areas with high vacationer interest.

Adjusting the monetary advantages of the travel industry with the need to safeguard Ole's territory requires reasonable the travel industry rehearses. Executing and implementing rules for dependable marine the travel industry, including the restriction of damaging practices and the advancement of eco-accommodating exercises, are fundamental for limiting the effect of the travel industry on Ole's submerged home.

Preservation Procedures: Supporting Ole's Environment for People in the future

Actually tending to human effects on Ole's living space requires exhaustive preservation procedures that draw in nearby networks, policymakers, and partners. Here are key ways to deal with support Ole's territory for people in the future:

1. **Marine Safeguarded Regions (MPAs): Protecting Essential Territories**
   The foundation and extension of Marine Safeguarded Regions (MPAs) assume a significant part in defending Ole's environment. MPAs manage human exercises, giving asylums where coral reefs can recuperate and flourish. By assigning regions where fishing, securing, and other possibly destructive exercises are limited, MPAs add to the conservation of crucial territories for Ole.

2. **Reasonable Fishing Works on: Adjusting Harvest and Preservation**
   Executing and upholding supportable fishing rehearses are fundamental for keeping up with the equilibrium of the clownfish local area and safeguarding Ole's environment. Guidelines that breaking point get sizes, safeguard key rearing regions, and screen the effect of fishing exercises add to the reasonable administration of marine assets. Schooling and effort endeavors focusing on neighborhood fishers bring issues to light about the significance of manageable practices.

3. **Contamination Anticipation and The board: Safeguarding Water Quality**
   Diminishing contamination requires a multi-layered approach, including waste decrease, worked on squander the board, and the implementation of ecological

guidelines. Public mindfulness missions can teach networks about the effect of contamination on Ole and coral reefs, encouraging a feeling of obligation for safeguarding marine conditions. Joint effort between state run administrations, businesses, and neighborhood networks is fundamental for successful contamination anticipation and the board.

4. **Environmental Change Relief: Tending to the Main drivers**
Worldwide endeavors to relieve environmental change are basic for saving Ole's natural surroundings. Backing for diminished fossil fuel byproducts, manageable energy practices, and environment strength drives can address the underlying drivers of environmental change. Nearby and global coordinated efforts are crucial for carry out systems that improve the versatile limit of coral biological systems, permitting Ole's territory to flourish in the midst of changing ecological circumstances.

5. **Reasonable The travel industry Works on: Adjusting Diversion and Protection**
Reasonable the travel industry rehearses are vital to limiting the effect of human exercises on Ole's territory. Executing and authorizing rules for mindful marine the travel industry, including the preclusion of damaging practices and the advancement of eco-accommodating exercises, add to protection endeavors. Drawing in neighborhood networks in the travel industry the executives guarantees that financial advantages are offset with the protection of Ole's environment.

6. **Exploration and Checking: Illuminating Proof Based Protection**
Consistent exploration drives zeroed in on Ole's natural surroundings, its biological connections, and reactions to ecological changes give fundamental information to prove based protection techniques. Logical examinations concerning the soundness of coral reefs, the versatility of Ole's natural surroundings, and the effects of preservation measures add to a more profound comprehension of the mind boggling elements at play. Observing projects that track changes in Ole's natural surroundings over the long run improve the versatile limit of preservation systems, guaranteeing their importance and adequacy.

7. **Local area Commitment and Schooling: Cultivating Stewardship**

Connecting with nearby networks and cultivating training are fundamental parts of preservation endeavors pointed toward safeguarding Ole's living space. By bringing issues to light about the exceptional qualities and natural significance of Ole's living space, preservationists engage networks to become advocates for reef stewardship. Instructive projects, outreach drives, and organizations with nearby partners add to building a feeling of obligation for the prosperity of Ole's natural surroundings and the more extensive marine environment.

5.3 Conservation Efforts and Future Strategies

Notwithstanding mounting dangers to Ole and its coral natural surroundings, coordinated protection endeavors have been started to shield this less popular types of clownfish. These undertakings envelop a scope of systems pointed toward relieving natural surroundings corruption, tending to environmental change influences, advancing economical practices, and drawing in neighborhood networks. As we ponder continuous protection endeavors, what's to come holds the commitment of imaginative techniques to guarantee the getting through presence of Ole in coral reef biological systems.

Current Preservation Drives: A Comprehensive Methodology

Current preservation drives center around both safeguarding Ole's environment and tending to more extensive difficulties confronting coral reefs. Marine Safeguarded Regions (MPAs) have arisen as basic devices for protecting fundamental environments, managing human exercises, and cultivating biological system strength. These assigned zones give safe-havens where Ole and its kindred reef occupants can flourish, undisturbed by unfavorable human effects.

Environmental change relief is a focal subject in protection endeavors, recognizing the worldwide idea of the danger. Promotion for decreased fossil fuel byproducts, reasonable energy practices, and environment versatility drives are in progress to mitigate the stressors presented by climbing ocean temperatures and sea fermentation. These endeavors intend to make conditions helpful for Ole's endurance inside its changing submerged home.

Feasible fishing practices and guidelines are crucial in keeping up with the fragile equilibrium of the clownfish local area. By advancing dependable fishing, restricting catch estimates, and safeguarding key rearing regions, progressives plan to guarantee that Ole's living space stays strong and fit for supporting sound populaces.

Future Methodologies: Advancements and Joint efforts

Looking forward, future techniques for Ole's protection will probably integrate state of the art advancements, creative exploration, and upgraded local area commitment. High level checking advancements, including submerged drones and hereditary examinations, offer chances to accumulate exact information on Ole's populace patterns, ways of behaving, and hereditary variety. These devices upgrade how we might interpret the species and illuminate designated preservation activities.

Long haul checking projects will keep on assuming an essential part in following populace drifts and assessing the viability of preservation mediations. By laying out a benchmark and following changes after some time, researchers can adjust techniques to address arising dangers and guarantee the determination of Ole in coral reef environments.

Local area contribution will stay a foundation of future protection methodologies. Enabling neighborhood networks through schooling, effort, and cooperation in checking endeavors encourages a feeling of responsibility and stewardship. By building organizations with the people who live in closeness to Ole's territory, progressives make an organization of devoted people pursuing shared objectives.

Worldwide cooperation is fundamental for tending to the transboundary idea of marine protection. By encouraging organizations between nations, specialists, and associations, a bound together methodology can be created to handle worldwide difficulties, for example, environmental change, contamination, and overfishing.

Chapter 6

Ole In Captivity

The appeal of Ole, the less popular types of clownfish, stretches out past the coral reefs to enrapture the hearts of aquarium devotees. As aquarium specialists look to bring a piece of the sea into their homes, the consideration and farming of Ole in bondage become focal contemplations. This investigation dives into the exceptional qualities of Ole, the difficulties of keeping a solid hostage climate, moral contemplations, and the potential for rearing projects that add to the preservation of this unlikely treasure of the reef.

Figuring out Ole's Novel Qualities in Imprisonment

Ole's enamoring presence in home aquariums originates from its particular highlights and ways of behaving. As an individual from the clownfish family, Ole displays energetic shading, with varieties that can go from profound oranges to rich tans. These striking tones, combined with the trademark designs on its body, make Ole a tastefully satisfying expansion to marine aquariums.

Ole's social nature and fascinating ways of behaving further improve its enticement for aquarium devotees. In the wild, clownfish, including Ole, structure harmonious associations with ocean anemones, looking for cover among their limbs. This conduct is many times reproduced in imprisonment, with Ole exhibiting special communications with anemones or fake designs copy their presence.

Understanding the natural requirements of Ole is urgent for giving a reasonable hostage climate. The species is firmly connected with coral reefs, and its prosperity in bondage relies upon imitating key parts of its normal environment, including proper water boundaries, substrate, and haven choices.

Difficulties of Keeping Ole in Imprisonment: Emulating the Reef Climate

While the appeal of keeping Ole in bondage is obvious, it accompanies innate difficulties. Effectively keeping up with Ole in an aquarium setting requires cautious consideration regarding its particular necessities, and deviations from its common habitat can prompt pressure, medical problems, and decreased life expectancy.

1. **Water Boundaries: Making progress toward Reef-like Circumstances**
   Repeating the water boundaries of Ole's regular territory is a perplexing errand. Keeping up with stable saltiness levels, temperature reaches, and pH values is fundamental for the wellbeing and prosperity of Ole.
   Also, the nature of water, including low smelling salts, nitrite, and nitrate levels, is significant. Accomplishing and supporting these boundaries require ordinary testing, constant water changes, and the utilization of cutting edge filtration frameworks.

2. **Tank Size and Design: Making a Coral Safe house**
   The size and design of the aquarium assume a significant part in Ole's prosperity. Clownfish, including Ole, are known for their regional ways of behaving and progressive designs inside gatherings. Giving more than adequate space, proper concealing spots, and designs that emulate coral developments are fundamental. The presentation of live stone and substrate that upholds the foundation of helpful microorganisms adds to a more normal and stable climate.

3. **Similarity and Social Elements: Exploring Clownfish People group**
   Clownfish are social animals, and Ole is no exemption. Notwithstanding, laying out and keeping up with viable networks in imprisonment can challenge. Forceful ways of behaving, especially during the presentation of new people, can prompt pressure and wounds. Cautious determination of tankmates and acclimatization processes are pivotal for encouraging an agreeable climate.

4. **Sustenance: Addressing Dietary Necessities**

Giving a healthfully adjusted diet is fundamental for Ole's wellbeing. In the wild, clownfish have a different eating routine that incorporates little shellfish, zooplankton, and green growth. In imprisonment, it is fundamental to reproduce this fluctuated diet. Excellent business food varieties, enhanced with periodic contributions of live or frozen food varieties, add to the general wellbeing and energy of Ole.

Moral Contemplations: Dependable Clownfish Keeping
The moral contemplations of keeping Ole in imprisonment rotate around dependable and manageable practices. As the interest for clownfish in the aquarium exchange proceeds, it is basic to guarantee that the assortment, transportation, and offer of Ole are directed morally and economically.

1. **Feasible Obtaining: Picking Hostage Reared Examples**
   One moral decision for aquarium aficionados is to settle on hostage reared Ole examples. Hostage reproducing programs assist with diminishing the effect of wild assortment on coral reef environments. Picking Ole that has been reproduced in bondage upholds maintainable practices and adds to the preservation of the species right at home.

2. **Mindfulness and Instruction: Encouraging Dependable Possession**
   Bringing issues to light about the particular requirements and ways of behaving of Ole is fundamental for encouraging mindful possession. Training drives, both for specialists and those engaged with the aquarium exchange, add to a more educated and upright way to deal with clownfish cultivation. Understanding the difficulties and responsibilities engaged with keeping Ole in imprisonment energizes mindful direction.

3. **Preservation Commitments: Supporting Rearing Projects**

Cooperation in or support for reproducing programs committed to clownfish, including Ole, is a significant way for aquarium devotees to add to preservation endeavors. These projects not just stock the market with capably reared examples yet in addition assume a part in exploration and protection drives zeroed in on the species' regular territory.

Rearing Ole in Imprisonment: A Way to Protection

Rearing Ole in imprisonment presents a double an open door: it fulfills the interest for aquarium examples while adding to the protection of wild populaces. Effective reproducing programs depend on a careful comprehension of Ole's regenerative ways of behaving, healthful necessities, and the complexities of larval raising.

1. **Romance and Match Holding: Emulating Normal Ways of behaving**
   Clownfish, including Ole, participate in complex romance customs and structure monogamous matches. Duplicating these normal ways of behaving in imprisonment includes giving proper designs to settling, making domains, and permitting matches to frame bonds. Noticing and regarding the pair holding process is pivotal for effective reproducing.

2. **Egg Assortment and Larval Raising: Sustaining the Future**
   When a couple of Ole has effectively laid eggs, cautious checking and intercession might be important for larval endurance. Gathering and raising clownfish hatchlings requires specific information, hardware, and commitment. Giving appropriate larval food sources, keeping up with ideal water conditions, and safeguarding the hatchlings from predation are basic parts of the raising system.

3. **Cooperation with Rearing Projects: Adding to Protection**

Aquarium fans keen on rearing Ole can team up with laid out reproducing programs. These projects frequently offer help, direction, and admittance to hereditarily different rearing matches. By taking part in such drives, specialists add to the hereditary variety of hostage populaces and backing more extensive preservation objectives.

6.1 Challenges and Opportunities of Keeping Ole in Aquariums

The charm of Ole, the less popular types of clownfish, coaxes aquarium fans to set out on an excursion of marine farming. Notwithstanding, the undertaking to keep Ole in aquariums presents a nuanced embroidery of difficulties and open doors. From mirroring the intricacy of its normal natural surroundings to addressing moral contemplations and adding to protection endeavors, the consideration of Ole in imprisonment requires a sensitive equilibrium and a pledge to capable stewardship.

Difficulties of Keeping Ole in Aquariums

1. **Natural surroundings Replication: Imitating the Reef Climate**

   Imitating the unpredictable reef climate that Ole occupies represents a critical test in imprisonment. Clownfish, including Ole, have explicit natural necessities, and deviations from these can prompt pressure and medical problems. Making a reasonable living space includes repeating coral developments, giving proper substrate, and guaranteeing the accessibility of designs that mirror the safe house given by anemones in nature.

   Keeping up with stable water boundaries, including saltiness, temperature, and pH, is essential. Accomplishing and supporting these boundaries require thorough observing, standard water changes, and the utilization of cutting edge filtration frameworks. The intricacy of Ole's regular living space requests a pledge to consistent learning and variation to give a flourishing climate.

2. **Tank Size and Design: Tending to Regional Ways of behaving**

   Clownfish, known for their regional ways of behaving, present difficulties as far as tank size and design. Ole lays out regions inside the aquarium, and giving adequate room is fundamental to forestall forceful ways of behaving and regional questions. Congestion can prompt pressure and expected damage to people.

   Establishing a dynamic and drawing in climate with reasonable concealing spots and designs helps address regional ways of behaving. Cautious thought of tank mates, particularly inside the clownfish local area, is crucial to cultivate an amicable concurrence.

3. **Social Elements: Exploring Clownfish People group**

   Understanding and dealing with the social elements inside a clownfish local area, including Ole, can challenge. Presenting new people might set off forceful ways of behaving and progressive difficulties. Cautious acclimatization and observing are important to guarantee the prosperity of all people in the aquarium.

   Adjusting the craving to grandstand the social idea of clownfish with the need to forestall hostility requires a nuanced approach. Species-explicit ways of behaving, orientation contemplations, and viable tank mates assume vital parts in forming a firm local area.

4. **Nourishment: Addressing Dietary Necessities**

   Giving a healthfully adjusted diet is fundamental for Ole's wellbeing in imprisonment. While clownfish are known to have a changed eating routine in the wild, recreating this variety can challenge. Great business food sources enhanced with live or frozen choices add to a reasonable eating routine.

   Guaranteeing that Ole gets fitting nourishment includes grasping its dietary inclinations and checking its taking care of ways of behaving. Overloading or dependence on a restricted eating regimen can prompt nourishing inadequacies and medical problems.

5. **Stress The executives: Limiting Natural Stressors**

Clownfish, including Ole, are delicate to natural stressors. Changes in water boundaries, disturbances in the tank climate, or the presence of forceful tank mates can actuate pressure. Persistent pressure debilitates the safe framework and makes Ole defenseless to sicknesses.

Moderating pressure includes keeping a steady and secure climate. Slow acclimatization to changes, limiting interruptions, and choosing viable tank mates add to pressure the board. Normal perception and brief reaction to indications of stress are significant parts of fruitful clownfish cultivation.

Chances of Keeping Ole in Aquariums

1. **Instructive Effort: Cultivating Mindfulness and Understanding**
   Saving Ole in aquariums gives a priceless open door to instructive effort. Aquarium lovers, especially the people who keep clownfish, become envoys for marine preservation. Sharing information about Ole's regular ways of behaving, biological significance, and the difficulties it faces in the wild cultivates mindfulness and understanding among specialists and the more extensive local area.
   Aquariums can act as stages for instructive projects, studios, and intuitive shows. By displaying the magnificence and intricacy of Ole's living space, aquariums add to the appreciation and preservation of coral reef environments. Instructive drives rouse a feeling of obligation for the prosperity of marine life and the protection of normal territories.

2. **Protection Commitments: Supporting Reproducing Projects**
   Partaking in or supporting reproducing programs committed to clownfish, including Ole, is a significant way for aquarium lovers to add to preservation endeavors. Hostage reproducing programs assume a vital part in lessening the interest for wild-got examples, mitigating tension on normal populaces.
   Aquarium specialists can team up with laid out reproducing programs, share their encounters, and add to the hereditary variety of hostage populaces. By partaking in such drives, they effectively support more extensive preservation objectives and add to the manageability of the aquarium exchange.

3. **Research Open doors: Progressing Clownfish Cultivation Information**
   Keeping Ole in aquariums opens ways to explore open doors that advance comprehension we might interpret clownfish cultivation. Perceptions of ways of behaving, conceptive elements, and reactions to ecological variables contribute significant information to the aggregate information base.
   Aquarium devotees, scientists, and establishments can team up to lead

concentrates on that benefit both hostage and wild populaces of clownfish. The bits of knowledge acquired from aquarium farming add to confirm based preservation techniques, informed rearing practices, and the general prosperity of clownfish in different conditions.

4. **Reproducing Achievement: Sustaining Hostage Populaces**

The fruitful reproducing of Ole in imprisonment is a critical chance for aquarium fans. Rearing projects add to the accessibility of capably reproduced examples in the aquarium exchange. Ole's effective multiplication in imprisonment fulfills the interest for aquarium examples as well as assumes a part in exploration and protection drives.

Aquarium specialists who make reproducing progress can share their encounters, procedures, and best practices with the local area. This trade of information adds to the refinement of rearing techniques, improves the achievement paces of hostage reproducing programs, and reinforces the general supportability of clownfish in bondage.

6.2 Breeding Ole in Captivity

Rearing Ole, the less popular types of clownfish, in bondage addresses a charming undertaking that consolidates logical request, preservation commitments, and the delight of seeing the lifecycle of these submerged pearls. As aquarium fans try to open the insider facts of Ole's generation, a multi-layered venture unfurls, enveloping romance ceremonies, egg laying, larval raising, and the potential for adding to more extensive protection endeavors.

Figuring out Ole's Regenerative Ways of behaving

Prior to digging into the complexities of rearing Ole in imprisonment, a basic comprehension of the species' regenerative ways of behaving is fundamental.

Clownfish, including Ole, are known for their one of a kind romance ceremonies and monogamous pair-holding. These ways of behaving are profoundly imbued right at home, where they structure cooperative associations with ocean anemones.

In imprisonment, impersonating the circumstances that animate these normal ways of behaving is pivotal for fruitful rearing. Ole ordinarily frames monogamous matches, with people participating in multifaceted romance moves and regional ways of behaving. These ways of behaving signal the preparation of the pair to bring forth, starting the conceptive cycle.

Making way for Reproducing: Impersonating Normal Circumstances

1. **Tank Climate: Making a Reasonable Territory**
   Establishing a reasonable rearing climate for Ole includes duplicating key parts of its normal territory. The aquarium ought to give more than adequate space to coordinate holding and romance ceremonies, as well as reasonable designs for egg affidavit. Mirroring the presence of anemones, whether genuine or counterfeit, can invigorate normal ways of behaving.

Satisfactory concealing spots and designs that look like coral developments add to the general prosperity of Ole and give fundamental components to fruitful rearing. The tank size, water boundaries, and by and large tank arrangement assume significant parts in establishing a favorable climate.

2. **Match Holding and Romance: Noticing Regular Ways of behaving**

Noticing Ole's normal ways of behaving, especially pair-holding and romance, is a preface to effective reproducing. At the point when people structure matches, they display explicit ways of behaving like swimming together, having a similar space, and taking part in common prepping. These activities connote the foundation of a couple bond.

Romance ceremonies include many-sided moves, where the male Ole grandstands his balances and endeavors to allure the female. The female answers with equal developments, demonstrating her openness to generating. Close perception of these ways of behaving permits aquarium fans to recognize the ideal time for reproducing endeavors.

Egg Laying and Treatment: The Summit of Romance

1. **Choosing Reasonable Settling Locales**
   When the pair-holding and romance stages are effectively explored, Ole plans for egg laying. In the wild, clownfish normally lay their eggs on level surfaces close to the foundation of anemones or other reasonable designs. In imprisonment, giving reasonable settling locales is pivotal for the outcome of the rearing system. Level surfaces, for example, shakes or concentrated rearing stages, act as ideal areas for Ole to store its eggs. The chose site ought to be very much safeguarded, permitting the eggs to stick safely and working with the resulting care and observing of the creating hatchlings.

2. **Egg Laying Interaction: A Fragile Movement**

The egg-laying process includes a sensitive movement between the male and female Ole. The female deliveries her eggs, and the male follows intently, treating them with his milt. The glue idea of the eggs guarantees their connection to the picked substrate.

During this cycle, the male Ole effectively takes part in protecting the eggs, fanning them with his pectoral balances to keep up with oxygen stream and avoid expected dangers. The pair's obligation to safeguarding the grip is a demonstration of the animal varieties' commitment to conceptive achievement.

Larval Raising: Supporting the Future

The progress from eggs to hatchlings denotes a basic stage in the rearing system. Larval raising requires careful consideration regarding water quality, sustenance, and ecological circumstances to guarantee the endurance and advancement of the youthful clownfish. Ole's hatchlings are especially sensitive and require particular consideration.

1. **Larval Tank Arrangement: Giving a Sustain Accommodating Climate**
   Making a different larval tank is a typical practice in clownfish rearing. The larval tank ought to be furnished with fitting filtration frameworks, temperature control, and reasonable lighting. Guaranteeing a steady and unblemished water climate is fundamental for the wellbeing and improvement of Ole's hatchlings. The utilization of particular larval-raising tanks with delicate water stream forestalls pressure and takes into account the exact administration of natural circumstances. Microalgae societies can be acquainted with give a characteristic food source to the creating hatchlings.

2. **Taking care of Hatchlings: Adjusting Nourishment and Development**
   Taking care of Ole's hatchlings is a fragile cycle that includes giving sustenance in a structure reasonable for their minuscule size. Infusoria, rotifers, and cop-epods are ordinarily utilized as starting food hotspots for clownfish hatchlings. These live food varieties offer fundamental supplements and backing the quick development and advancement of the youthful fish.
   As the hatchlings develop, progressing to bigger live or arranged food varieties becomes fundamental. Offering a fluctuated and healthfully adjusted diet is urgent for advancing solid turn of events and guaranteeing the effective trans-formation of hatchlings into adolescent clownfish.

3. **Transformation and Settlement: A Groundbreaking Excursion**

Transformation denotes the extraordinary excursion from larval structure to ado-lescent clownfish. During this interaction, the hatchlings go through critical morpho-logical changes, including the improvement of trademark markings and highlights. Transformation regularly comes full circle in the settlement of adolescent clownfish, where they embrace a benthic way of life.

Giving appropriate substrate and asylum choices in the larval tank upholds the settlement cycle. The effective progress to a benthic presence implies the finishing of the larval raising stage and the development of adolescent Ole.

Adding to Protection Endeavors: The Job of Hostage Rearing

1. **Lessening Strain on Wild Populaces**
   Hostage rearing projects, including those zeroed in on Ole, assume a critical part in lessening the tension on wild populaces. The aquarium exchange has gener-ally depended on wild-gotten examples, adding to environment corruption and populace decline. The outcome of hostage reproducing drives eases this strain and advances manageability.

2. **Hereditary Variety and Versatility**
   Hostage rearing adds to hereditary variety inside hostage populaces of Ole. Keeping a different genetic stock is fundamental for the drawn out strength and wellbeing of hostage populaces. Capable rearing works on, including endeavors to keep away from inbreeding, assist with saving the species' hereditary honesty.

3. **Examination and Protection Coordinated effort**

Hostage rearing projects frequently act as stages for research joint effort between aquarium lovers, analysts, and traditionalists. The experiences acquired from rearing Ole in imprisonment add to a more profound comprehension of the species' science, ways of behaving, and regenerative elements.

Cooperative endeavors stretch out past the limits of aquariums and benefit more extensive preservation drives. Research discoveries illuminate preservation procedures, living space security measures, and drives pointed toward safeguarding the regular natural surroundings of clownfish, including Ole.

Challenges in Reproducing Ole in Bondage

While the possibility of reproducing Ole in bondage holds guarantee, it accompanies inborn difficulties that request cautious thought and devotion.

1. **Complex Regenerative Ways of behaving**
   The many-sided romance and conceptive ways of behaving of Ole present difficulties for fruitful reproducing. Understanding the subtleties of pair-holding, romance moves, and ideal generating conditions requires sharp perception and a nuanced way to deal with tank the executives.

2. **Larval Raising Trouble**
   Larval raising is a sensitive stage where the endurance of Ole's posterity remains in a precarious situation. Giving proper nourishment, keeping up with ideal water conditions, and dealing with the change from live to arranged food sources present continuous difficulties.

3. **Moral Contemplations**

Reproducing Ole in bondage raises moral contemplations connected with the capable responsibility for. The interest for hostage reproduced examples shouldn't coincidentally add to overexploitation or unscrupulous rearing practices. Supporting drives that focus on the prosperity of clownfish and add to more extensive protection objectives is fundamental.

6.3 Responsible Ownership and Conservation through Aquariums

Aquariums, when drawn closer with a guarantee to dependable possession and preservation, act as amazing assets for cultivating marine mindfulness and stewardship. The enthralling charm of submerged biological systems brought into homes empowers lovers to see the value in the excellence of marine life as well as contribute definitively to the safeguarding of sea-going conditions. In this investigation, we dive into the standards of capable proprietorship, the instructive capability of aquariums, their part in preservation, and the moral contemplations that guide the feasible acts of aquarium devotees.

Standards of Mindful Possession

1. **Moral Obtainment of Marine Life**

   Mindful possession starts with the moral acquisition of marine life for aquariums. Picking reasonably obtained and hostage reared examples, as opposed to depending on wild-gotten people, diminishes the effect on regular populaces. Supporting organizations and drives that focus on moral practices in the aquarium exchange adds to the prosperity of marine environments.

2. **Insightful Tank Plan and Upkeep**

   Making a reasonable and maintainable living space inside aquariums is a major part of capable possession. Insightful tank configuration thinks about the particular requirements of the occupants, including proper tank size, reasonable substrate, and designs that imitate common habitats. Ordinary upkeep, like water quality testing and appropriate filtration, guarantees the wellbeing and prosperity of the oceanic local area.

3. **Informed Species Choice**

   The choice of species for aquariums ought to be directed by exhaustive examination and thought of their natural necessities. Aficionados ought to pick species that are appropriate to bondage, taking into account factors, for example, tank size, similarity with different species, and dietary prerequisites. Keeping away from species with specific requirements or those inclined to pressure in bondage adds to mindful possession.

4. **Capable Reproducing Practices**

   For those participated in reproducing programs, capable practices are fundamental. Reproducing ought to focus on hereditary variety, keep away from inbreeding, and add to the general wellbeing of hostage populaces. Rearing projects can assume a pivotal part in protection endeavors, particularly for species confronting dangers in nature.

5. **Support for Protection Drives**

Capable proprietorship reaches out past the bounds of individual aquariums to incorporate dynamic help for protection drives. Devotees can add to marine preservation through monetary help, cooperation in research projects, and commitment to local area put together drives centered with respect to protecting regular environments.

Instructive Capability of Aquariums

1. **Associating Individuals with Marine Life**
   Aquariums act as vivid windows into the entrancing universe of marine life, permitting individuals to interface with species they may very well never experience in nature. From dynamic coral reefs to the perplexing ways of behaving of fish, aquariums give an unmistakable and charming instructive experience.

2. **Motivating Interest and Learning**
   The dynamic and various environments inside aquariums rouse interest and learning. Noticing the ways of behaving of marine occupants, figuring out their natural jobs, and investigating the complexities of life underneath the waves encourage a more profound appreciation for the intricacy of marine environments.

3. **Advancing Protection Education**
   Aquariums assume a fundamental part in advancing preservation education by bringing issues to light about the difficulties looked by marine conditions. Displays that feature issues like coral dying, overfishing, and natural surroundings obliteration add to an additional educated and ecologically cognizant public.

4. **Empowering Dependable Way of behaving**

Training through aquariums goes past information procurement; it supports mindful way of behaving. Guests gain bits of knowledge into the fragile equilibrium between marine environments and the effect of human activities. This information engages people to settle on informed decisions that line up with the standards of marine protection.

Aquariums as Protection Apparatuses

1. **Ex Situ Protection**
   Aquariums act as significant devices for ex situ preservation, protecting species that face dangers in their regular natural surroundings. By keeping up with hostage populaces, aquariums go about as protection against the possible loss of biodiversity in nature. Species reared in bondage might possibly be once again introduced to their local surroundings to support lessening populaces.

2. **Exploration and Protection Joint effort**
   Aquariums frequently team up with scientists and protection associations to contribute important information and experiences. Concentrates on led inside the controlled climate of aquariums furnish analysts with amazing chances to all the more likely grasp the science, conduct, and biology of marine species. This information is fundamental for illuminating preservation methodologies and territory assurance measures.

3. **Species Recuperation Projects**
   Some aquariums effectively partake in species recuperation programs for fundamentally jeopardized species. By reproducing and keeping up with populaces of imperiled species, these projects mean to forestall their annihilation and add to

more extensive protection drives. The effective renewed introduction of hostage reared people to their normal natural surroundings is a demonstration of the viability of such projects.

4. **Public Commitment and Backing**

Aquariums have the ability to prepare public commitment and backing for marine protection. Through instructive projects, outreach drives, and intelligent shows, aquariums move guests to become advocates for the security of seas and the existence they maintain. This aggregate support adds to more extensive endeavors focused on approach change and feasible practices.

Moral Contemplations in Aquarium Possession

1. **Protection Over Assortment**
   Devotees ought to focus on the preservation of species over their assortment for individual aquariums. Picking species that are not under danger and supporting maintainable practices in the aquarium exchange line up with moral contemplations. Preservation cognizant decisions add to the general strength of marine biological systems.

2. **Evasion of Obtrusive Species**
   The unexpected arrival of aquarium species into normal territories represents a huge danger to neighborhood environments. Mindful possession incorporates the evasion of species that can possibly become intrusive whenever delivered. Appropriate removal techniques for undesirable aquarium occupants are fundamental to forestall environmental disturbances.

3. **Maintainable Practices in the Exchange**
   Aquarium lovers ought to effectively uphold organizations that stick to manageable practices in the exchange. This incorporates obtaining marine life dependably, focusing on hostage reared examples, and keeping away from rehearses that add to natural surroundings corruption or double-dealing of wild populaces.

4. **Sympathy and Prosperity of Hostage Creatures**

Moral contemplations reach out to the compassion and prosperity of the creatures kept in bondage. Aficionados ought to focus on the wellbeing and solace of their aquarium occupants, giving reasonable conditions that mirror normal circumstances. This incorporates offering proper concealing spots, a fluctuated and nutritious eating regimen, and limiting pressure prompting factors.

Chapter 7

Unraveling Ole's Mysteries

In the huge spread of coral reefs, where a variety of marine life paints the sea with lively shades, Ole, the less popular types of clownfish, conceals its secrets underneath the waves. As aquarium lovers and scientists the same look to unwind the privileged insights of Ole's confounding presence, an excursion into its biological specialty, transformative history, and novel social qualities divulges an embroidery of interest and interest.

Environmental Specialty of Ole: Where Privileged insights Dwell

1. **Geographic Dissemination and Territory Inclination**

   Ole, logically delegated Amphiprion oleanus, occupies explicit areas of the Indo-Pacific, with its reach stretching out from the banks of northern Australia to the islands of Melanesia. Inside this far reaching an area, Ole looks for asylum in the haven of coral reefs, shaping harmonious associations with ocean anemones.

   The coral reefs give Ole an actual shelter as well as a different and plentiful environment. The complex designs of the reefs offer concealing spots, favorable places, and searching open doors, making an interconnected snare of life where Ole's insider facts unfurl.

2. **Favored Reef Conditions**

Digging into Ole's favored reef conditions uncovers a nuanced relationship with the coral designs. Ole is frequently connected with explicit microhabitats inside the reef, floating towards regions with a blend of live corals, anemones, and reasonable substrates for settling. Understanding the complexities of these favored conditions gives bits of knowledge into the species' environmental necessities and ways of behaving.

Developmental History: Following Ole's Tribal Roots

1. **Lineage inside the Clownfish Family**

   Ole has a place with the sweeping group of clownfish, experimentally known as Pomacentridae. The transformative history of clownfish follows back large number of years, exhibiting their versatility and flexibility in marine conditions. Ole, as an individual from this different family, conveys the hereditary tradition of its predecessors, formed by the unique powers of development.

2. **Transformative Variations to Reef Life**

   The developmental transformations of Ole mirror its specialization in reef life. Throughout the span of ages, clownfish, including Ole, have created extraordinary highlights and ways of behaving that improve their endurance inside the complicated biological systems of coral reefs. These variations incorporate particular hue for cover, advantageous associations with anemones, and many-sided social designs inside their networks.

3. **Coevolution with Ocean Anemones**

One of the getting through secrets of Ole lies in its coevolutionary relationship with ocean anemones. While the stinging limbs of anemones dissuade most fish, clownfish, including Ole, have fostered an exceptional invulnerability to these poisons. This coevolutionary variation permits Ole to look for shelter among the limbs of anemones, acquiring security from hunters and framing a remarkable and commonly helpful organization.

Actual Attributes: The Visual Verse of Ole

1. **Particular Hue and Examples**

   Ole's actual appearance is a visual verse that unfurls inside the coral reefs. The species displays a range of varieties going from dynamic oranges to rich earthy colors, decorated with particular examples that change among people. Unwinding the explanations for Ole's striking shading opens a window into its correspondence techniques, mate choice, and job inside the complex embroidery of reef life.

2. **Size and Morphological Highlights**

Investigating Ole's size and morphological elements uncovers the complexities of its transformations for life in coral conditions. Clownfish, as a rule, are described by their little size, horizontally compacted bodies, and a defensive layer of bodily fluid that keeps them from being stung by the anemones they occupy. Ole's size and morphology mirror a sensitive harmony between mobility inside the reef structures and the requirement for insurance.

Conduct Qualities: Disentangling the Social Elements of Ole

1. **Social Design inside Clownfish People group**

   The social elements of Ole inside clownfish networks are an area of significant interest. Clownfish structure progressive social designs with a predominant reproducing pair at the top. Unwinding the complexities of Ole's social ways of behaving, specialized techniques, and the jobs played by various people inside the gathering gives a brief look into the helpful methodologies that add to the local area's endurance.

2. **Interesting Settling and Rearing Propensities**

Ole's settling and reproducing propensities are a riddle inside the domain of clownfish ways of behaving. The development of monogamous matches, the fastidious choice of settling destinations, and the cooperative consideration of posterity grandstand the species' obligation to regenerative achievement. Understanding the variables impacting settling ways of behaving and the intricacies of mate choice reveals insight into the transformative meaning of these customs.

Natural surroundings and Environment: Ole's Job in the Coral Biological system

1. **Coral Reef Biological system Elements**
   Ole, as other clownfish species, assumes an imperative part in the elements of coral reef biological systems. Its communications with anemones, the formation of settling destinations, and rummaging ways of behaving add to the wellbeing and equilibrium of the reef. Unwinding Ole's biological job gives important bits of knowledge into the interconnected connections that shape the biodiversity and flexibility of coral environments.

2. **Connection with Other Marine Species**

Past its connections with anemones, Ole participates in complex associations with other marine species. From cleaning beneficial interaction with different reef occupants to expected clashes with regional neighbors, Ole's collaborations structure a mind boggling snare of environmental elements. Understanding the complexities of these connections adds to an all encompassing perception of Ole's environmental impression.

Preservation Status and Dangers: Defending Ole's Future

1. **Evaluation of Protection Status**
   The protection status of Ole is an essential thought in unwinding its secrets. Evaluating the populace patterns, dispersion, and potential dangers looked by the species gives an establishment to protection endeavors. Ole's status might shift across its reach, and an exhaustive comprehension is fundamental for focused on and viable protection drives.

2. **Assessment of Populace Patterns**

Assessing Ole's populace patterns includes investigating variables like territory debasement, overfishing, and environmental change. By unwinding the mind boggling exchange of these dangers, specialists and progressives can distinguish areas of weakness and carry out procedures to alleviate populace declines. The evaluation of populace patterns is a critical part of Ole's protection story.

Human Effect on Ole's Environment: Adjusting Presence and Protection

1. **Anthropogenic Dangers to Coral Reefs**
   The secrets of Ole's territory are entwined with the effect of human exercises on coral reefs. Anthropogenic dangers, for example, overfishing, natural surroundings annihilation, and environmental change present critical difficulties to Ole's endurance. Understanding the extension and ramifications of these dangers is fundamental for planning preservation estimates that address the underlying drivers of environment corruption.

2. **Maintainable Practices for Coral Reef Security**

Offsetting human presence with the safeguarding of Ole's living space requires a guarantee to manageable practices. Protection drives that advance feasible fishing, living space rebuilding, and environmental change relief add to the drawn out well-being of coral reefs. Unwinding the intricacies of human effect on Ole's environment directs the advancement of systems that cultivate concurrence with marine biological systems.

Protection Endeavors and Future Techniques: Graphing a Course for Ole's Prosperity

1. **Cooperative Preservation Drives**
   Preservation endeavors for Ole blossom with coordinated effort between scientists, protection associations, and nearby networks. Laying out associations that influence logical skill, local area commitment, and strategy support improves the adequacy of protection drives. Unwinding the intricacies of Ole's preservation requires a multi-faceted methodology that tends to both prompt dangers and hidden issues.

2. **Reconciliation of Logical Exploration**
   Logical examination is a key part in the protection of Ole. Unwinding its secrets requires progressing investigation into its science, ways of behaving, and natural prerequisites. Incorporating logical discoveries into protection methodologies guarantees that drives are educated by proof based works on, prompting more powerful and designated intercessions.

3. **Training and Effort for Marine Stewardship**

Training and effort programs assume a urgent part in disentangling Ole's secrets for the more extensive public. Cultivating marine stewardship through mindfulness crusades, local area commitment, and instructive drives imparts a feeling of obligation for the prosperity of Ole and its living space. The joining of marine protection into instructive educational programs makes an establishment for people in the future focused on saving marine biodiversity.

7.1 Ongoing Research and Knowledge Gaps

While steps have been made in understanding the complicated universe of Ole, the less popular types of clownfish, there stay huge information holes and progressing research attempts that enamor the consideration of researchers, sea life scholars, and aquarium devotees. The quest for information about Ole stretches out from its biological specialty to its ways of behaving, developmental history, and the difficulties it faces in changing marine conditions.

1. **Natural Elements and Cooperations**
   Conduct Environment inside Clownfish People group
   A major part of progressing research includes diving into the conduct biology of Ole inside clownfish networks. Grasping the subtleties of social connections, correspondence techniques, and helpful ways of behaving among people adds to an exhaustive image of Ole's job inside the coral reef environment. Scientists try to disentangle the complexities of how clownfish networks, including Ole, explore progressive designs and keep up with amicable connections.
   Effect of Ole on Coral Reef Wellbeing
   The more extensive environmental elements including Ole and its effect on coral reef wellbeing are areas of dynamic examination. Researchers are investigating the species' scavenging propensities, expected jobs as reef cleaners through harmonious communications, and commitments to supplement cycling inside the environment. Unwinding these perspectives gives experiences into the biological administrations Ole offers and its importance in keeping up with the equilibrium of coral reef conditions.

2. **Regenerative Science and Reproducing Procedures**
   Mating Frameworks and Conceptive Achievement
   Progressing examination into Ole's conceptive science means to unwind the complexities of its mating frameworks and elements affecting regenerative achievement. Exploring the systems behind mate choice, romance ceremonies, and the foundation of monogamous matches gives significant experiences into the species' transformative procedures. Specialists are quick to comprehend how these conceptive ways of behaving add to the drawn out endurance and hereditary variety of Ole populaces.
   Larval Raising and Endurance Difficulties
   The excursion from eggs to hatchlings denotes a basic stage in Ole's life cycle, and specialists are effectively investigating the difficulties looked during larval

raising. Examining factors affecting larval endurance, dietary prerequisites, and the progress to adolescent stages reveals insight into the weakness of Ole's posterity.

Understanding these perspectives is critical for creating preservation techniques that help the whole lifecycle of the species.

3. **Developmental History and Hereditary Variety**

Hereditary Variety and Populace Hereditary qualities

Unwinding Ole's developmental history includes digging into its hereditary variety and populace hereditary qualities. Specialists are leading examinations to evaluate the hereditary changeability inside various populaces of Ole. Understanding the conveyance of hereditary variety illuminates preservation endeavors by recognizing hereditarily particular gatherings and potential protection units. It additionally supports alleviating the dangers related with inbreeding and populace declines.

Phylogenetic Connections inside Clownfish

The more extensive setting of Ole's phylogenetic connections inside the clownfish family stays a continuous area of investigation. Scientists plan to explain how Ole squeezes into the developmental tree of clownfish species, distinguishing shared family line and extraordinary variations. Similar phylogenetics adds to a more profound comprehension of Ole's developmental direction and its associations with different individuals from the Pomacentridae family.

4. **Environmental Change Strength and Variation**

Effect of Environmental Change on Ole's Natural surroundings

As coral reefs face the extraordinary difficulties of environmental change, continuous exploration examines how Ole's natural surroundings is being influenced. Increasing ocean temperatures, sea fermentation, and outrageous climate occasions present dangers to coral reefs, possibly influencing Ole's dissemination, conduct, and in general endurance. Researchers are attempting to translate the particular stressors and potential transformations that might impact Ole in an evolving environment.

Versatility Procedures and Preservation Measures

Investigating Ole's flexibility techniques despite natural stressors is a key concentration. Scientists try to recognize systems that might present versatility to environment instigated changes, like warm resistance or versatile ways of behaving. This information illuminates preservation measures pointed toward improving the species' capacity to endure the difficulties presented by a quickly changing marine climate.

5. **Correspondence and Social Elements**

Correspondence Modalities inside Clownfish People group

The correspondence modalities inside clownfish networks, including Ole, are subjects of progressing research. Researchers are disentangling the complexities of visual signs, substance prompts, and acoustic correspondence utilized by clownfish for intra-and interspecies communications. Understanding how Ole conveys inside its gathering improves our cognizance of the agreeable ways of behaving that characterize clownfish networks.

Job of Correspondence in Regional Ways of behaving

Regional ways of behaving among clownfish, including Ole, include complicated correspondence methodologies. Progressing research expects to unravel the job of correspondence in laying out and keeping up with regions inside the reef. Experiences into what correspondence means for pecking orders, mate determination, and helpful exercises give a more nuanced comprehension of Ole's social elements.

6. **Human-Ole Associations and Preservation**

Moral Practices in Aquarium Possession

The human-Ole communication inside the setting of aquarium proprietorship brings up issues about moral practices. Continuous exploration investigates the effects of the aquarium exchange on Ole populaces, stressing the significance of mindful proprietorship. Researchers and preservationists are attempting to depict rules for moral obtainment, reproducing rehearses, and the mindful consideration of Ole in imprisonment.

Public Mindfulness and Protection Support

Research attempts stretch out to assessing the viability of public mindfulness missions and protection backing endeavors. Understanding the elements that impact public view of Ole and its protection status helps tailor outreach drives. Continuous exploration in this domain means to overcome any barrier between logical information and public commitment, encouraging an aggregate obligation to the conservation of Ole and its environment.

7.2 Questions for Future Study

As how we might interpret Ole, the less popular types of clownfish, keeps on developing, the investigation of unknown waters uncovers a huge number of inquiries that coax future review. These inquiries range different features of Ole's presence — from its natural complexities to its conceptive secrets, transformative elements, and communications with an evolving climate.

In the mission for information, specialists and lovers the same dig into these inquiries, each addressing a gateway to more profound experiences and a more noteworthy comprehension of Ole's cryptic domain.

1. **Environmental Outskirts: Grasping Ole's Territory Elements**
   1.1 How does Ole add to coral reef strength?
   Investigating the perplexing connection among Ole and coral reefs reveals the likely commitments of this species to the flexibility of these sensitive environments. Specialists are quick to comprehend how Ole's ways of behaving, like

its collaborations with anemones and rummaging exercises, impact the well-being and strength of coral reefs. Disentangling these elements can illuminate preservation techniques zeroed in on protecting Ole as well as the whole reef environment.

1.2 What microhabitat inclinations does Ole show inside coral reefs?

Researching Ole's microhabitat inclinations inside coral reefs gives important bits of knowledge into the particular circumstances that cultivate its prosperity. Grasping the subtleties of Ole's environment choice, like its partiality for particular sorts of corals or explicit profundities, adds to designated protection endeavors and natural surroundings conservation drives.

1.3 How does Ole explore and adjust to changing reef conditions?

As coral reefs face extraordinary difficulties because of environmental change and human exercises, understanding how Ole explores and adjusts to changing conditions is essential. Scientists are digging into the species' capacity to adapt to variables like climbing ocean temperatures, sea fermentation, and territory debasement. Unwinding these transformations can direct protection measures pointed toward defending Ole notwithstanding progressing ecological changes.

2. **Conceptive Puzzlers: Interpreting Ole's Reproducing Systems**

   2.1 What variables impact mate determination and match holding in Ole?

   The complexities of mate choice and match holding in Ole address an enrapturing region for future review. Specialists look to disentangle the elements that impact these basic regenerative ways of behaving, investigating the job of viewable prompts, synthetic signs, and ecological circumstances in the arrangement and solidness of monogamous matches.

   2.2 How does Ole's regenerative achievement shift across various reef conditions?

   Looking at the variety in Ole's regenerative accomplishment across various reef conditions reveals insight into the species' versatility and environmental adaptability. Factors, for example, asset accessibility, contest for settling destinations, and predation dangers can impact the conceptive results for Ole. Understanding these varieties adds to a nuanced comprehension of the species' regenerative procedures.

   2.3 What are the larval endurance components utilized by Ole?

   The excursion from eggs to hatchlings is a basic stage in Ole's lifecycle, and scientists are fascinated by the endurance systems utilized during this weak stage. Exploring the species' transformations for larval endurance, including taking care of procedures, physiological changes, and environment inclinations, gives fundamental information to both preservation and hostage rearing projects.

3. **Developmental Enigmas: Following Ole's Tribal Pathways**

   3.1 How does Ole's developmental history add to its biological specialty?

   Unwinding Ole's developmental history discloses the pathways that have molded its environmental specialty. Scientists are investigating what the species' heritage has meant for its ways of behaving, physiological variations, and associations inside the coral reef environment. Following Ole's transformative pathways gives a more extensive setting to grasping its part in marine conditions.

3.2 What are the hereditary markers of flexibility in Ole populaces?

As Ole faces the difficulties presented by natural changes, distinguishing hereditary markers related with strength turns into a squeezing question. Analysts expect to reveal the hereditary varieties inside Ole populaces that present strength to stressors like temperature vacillations, illness episodes, and changes in food accessibility. This information illuminates protection systems zeroed in on saving hereditarily tough people.

3.3 How does Ole's phylogenetic position contrast with other clownfish species?

Similar phylogenetics offers a window into Ole's place inside the more extensive setting of clownfish development. Scientists are investigating the way that Ole's phylogenetic position looks at to other clownfish species, revealing insight into shared heritage, dissimilar developmental directions, and potential transformations extraordinary to Ole.

4. **Conduct Intricacies: Unraveling Ole's Social Elements**

4.1 Which jobs do individual clownfish play inside Ole's social construction?

Unwinding Ole's social elements includes investigating the jobs played by individual clownfish inside its local area. Scientists are digging into the ways of behaving of predominant people, subordinate individuals, and expected assistants with regards to rearing and regional safeguard. Understanding the complexities of these jobs adds to a thorough perspective on Ole's social design.

4.2 How do correspondence procedures add to Ole's people group cognizance?

Correspondence is a foundation of clownfish networks, and scientists are anxious to unravel how correspondence methodologies add to Ole's people group rationality. Exploring visual signs, synthetic signals, and potential acoustic correspondence reveals insight into the systems that work with participation, coordination, and data sharing inside Ole's gathering.

4.3 What is the effect of natural stressors on Ole's way of behaving?

As marine conditions face expanding pressure from anthropogenic and regular variables, understanding the effect of these stressors on Ole's way of behaving becomes central. Specialists are investigating how factors like contamination, commotion, and territory aggravations impact Ole's scavenging, reproducing, and social ways of behaving. Unwinding these impacts gives experiences into the species' strength and expected weaknesses.

5. **Environmental Change Strength: Systems for Ole's Endurance**

5.1 What are the versatile methodologies utilized by Ole because of environmental change?

With environmental change representing a critical danger to marine biological systems, specialists are examining the versatile techniques utilized by Ole to adapt to changing ecological circumstances. Looking at possible changes in conveyance, modifications in conduct, and physiological variations gives essential data to creating preservation methodologies that upgrade Ole's versatility in a quickly impacting world.

5.2 How could protection endeavors be custom fitted to address environment related dangers to Ole?

Fitting preservation endeavors to address environment related dangers is a vital inquiry for future review. Analysts are attempting to foster systems that alleviate the effects of environmental change on Ole and its territory. This incorporates distinguishing and safeguarding environment strong regions, executing natural surroundings rebuilding drives, and investigating imaginative ways to deal with environment transformation inside hostage populaces.

5.3 What is the job of Ole in advancing coral reef recuperation even with environment stress?

As coral reefs face the double difficulties of environmental change and different stressors, understanding the possible job of Ole in advancing recuperation becomes urgent. Specialists are investigating whether Ole's ways of behaving, for example, settling exercises and collaborations with anemones, add to the rebuilding of coral reef environments. Disentangling this biological riddle gives significant experiences into the interconnected connections that shape the strength of marine conditions.

6. Preservation Systems: Connecting Information Holes for Ole's Insurance

6.1 How might public commitment and schooling be advanced for Ole's preservation?

Improving public commitment and training is fundamental for accumulating support for Ole's protection. Specialists are investigating successful procedures for conveying logical information, cultivating compassion, and rousing activity among different crowds. Understanding the variables that impact public view of Ole adds to the improvement of significant protection correspondence drives.

6.2 Which job does Ole play in local area based preservation endeavors?

Local area based preservation drives are progressively perceived as significant for the security of marine conditions. Scientists are researching the job that Ole can play in such drives, investigating the potential for nearby networks to become stewards of Ole's territory. Cooperative endeavors that incorporate logical information with conventional biological insight add to comprehensive protection draws near.

6.3 How could moral practices in the aquarium exchange be upgraded for Ole's advantage?

The moral components of the aquarium exchange, especially comparable to Ole, warrant centered request. Specialists are inspecting ways of upgrading moral practices, diminish the effect of the exchange on wild populaces, and advance dependable proprietorship. Finding some kind of harmony between the aquarium leisure activity and protection goals is basic for guaranteeing Ole's prosperity both right at home and in bondage.

7.3 Collaborative Efforts in Clownfish Conservation

Clownfish, including the less popular Ole (Amphiprion oleanus), possess the multifaceted environments of coral reefs, dazzling marine aficionados and specialists the same. As these species face dangers from environmental change, territory corruption, and over-abuse, cooperative endeavors in clownfish protection have become central.

This cooperative methodology includes a collaboration of logical examination, local area commitment, and global participation to guarantee the conservation of these perplexing species.

Logical Joint effort: Disentangling Secrets for Preservation

Logical cooperation shapes the foundation of endeavors to preserve clownfish species, including Ole. Specialists from different fields like sea life science, nature, hereditary qualities, and climatology meet up to direct thorough investigations on the science, conduct, and biological jobs of clownfish. Through cooperative examination drives, established researchers expects to unwind the secrets encompassing clownfish, giving fundamental information to informed protection systems.

Logical cooperation stretches out to the observing of clownfish populaces, surveying their circulation, regenerative achievement, and reactions to ecological stressors. Long haul studies contribute important information that permits researchers to follow populace patterns, recognize key territories, and comprehend the effect of human exercises on clownfish environments.

Besides, worldwide coordinated efforts work with the sharing of examination discoveries and strategies, encouraging a worldwide comprehension of clownfish protection. Joint examination endeavors, information sharing stages, and cooperative distributions empower researchers to pool their mastery, making an aggregate information base that rises above geological limits.

Local area Commitment: Enabling Nearby Stewards

Protection endeavors for clownfish stretch out past the logical domain, embracing the dynamic cooperation of nearby networks. Cooperative drives enable seaside networks close clownfish territories to become stewards of these marine biological systems. Drawing in with nearby occupants through instructive projects, local area based undertakings, and effort exercises upgrades mindfulness about the significance of clownfish preservation.

Cooperative people group endeavors frequently remember preparing programs for feasible fishing rehearses, dependable the travel industry, and the foundation of marine safeguarded regions. By including neighborhood occupants in the protection cycle, networks become advocates for the safeguarding of clownfish environments, cultivating a feeling of pride and obligation.

In districts where the aquarium exchange represents an expected danger to clownfish populaces, cooperative endeavors draw in with nearby fishers and brokers. Maintainable gathering rehearses, hydroponics projects, and certificate plans are created cooperatively to work out some kind of harmony between the interest for clownfish in the aquarium exchange and the need to safeguard wild populaces.

Global Partnerships: A Brought together Front for Preservation

Clownfish protection benefits from worldwide collusions that unite legislatures, non-administrative associations (NGOs), and preservation organizations. These partnerships give a stage to the trading of thoughts, assets, and cooperative drives on a worldwide scale.

Worldwide associations add to the advancement of preservation arrangements and procedures that rise above political lines. Joint drives might incorporate the making of transboundary marine safeguarded regions, the foundation of preservation passages, and the execution of guidelines to control unlawful exchange and horrendous fishing rehearses.

Also, global subsidizing instruments support cooperative activities pointed toward saving clownfish natural surroundings. By pooling assets and ability, worldwide collusions can address complex difficulties, for example, environmental change, which requires composed endeavors to relieve its effect on clownfish and their biological systems.

Aquarium Industry Cooperation: Adjusting Preservation and Request

The aquarium business assumes a urgent part in clownfish protection, given the fame of these species among aquarium lovers. Cooperative endeavors inside the business center around advancing moral practices, economical obtaining, and dependable proprietorship.

Aquarium offices and fans team up with protection associations to bring issues to light about the possible effects of the exchange on wild clownfish populaces. This incorporates upholding for hostage reproducing programs, adherence to moral rules, and the advancement of aquacultured clownfish over wild-gotten examples.

Moreover, cooperative drives inside the aquarium business include the sharing of best practices for rearing and keeping up with clownfish in imprisonment. This trade of information adds to the improvement of fruitful reproducing programs, lessening the interest for wild-got examples and easing strain on normal populaces.

Difficulties and Open doors in Cooperative Protection

While cooperative endeavors in clownfish protection hold guarantee, they additionally face difficulties that require cautious route. Issues like changing preservation needs among partners, restricted financing, and varying administrative systems can block the viability of cooperative drives. Spanning these holes requires progressing correspondence, tact, and a common obligation to the overall objective of preservation.

Open doors for cooperation lie in utilizing mechanical progressions for information sharing, using resident science drives, and cultivating interdisciplinary methodologies.

Incorporating different viewpoints, including those of nearby networks and industry partners, guarantees a comprehensive comprehension of the difficulties looked by clownfish and works with the improvement of comprehensive protection techniques.